The Gibraltar Brigade on East Cemetery Hill

Twenty-Five Minutes of Fighting

The Gibraltar Brigade on East Cemetery Hill

Fifty Years of Controversy

Gettysburg • July 2, 1863

by

Gary G. Lash

**Butternut and Blue
1995**

First Edition

Copyright 1995 by Gary G. Lash

All rights reserved by the publisher. No part of this book may be reproduced in any form or by any method without permission in writing from the publisher.

ISBN 0-935523-50-2

Printed in the United States of America
on acid-free paper.

BUTTERNUT AND BLUE
3411 Northwind Road
Baltimore, Maryland 21234
410-256-9220

This first edition is limited to 1,000 copies.

DEDICATION

To my parents, George and Ruth Lash.

They taught me the important lessons.

TABLE OF CONTENTS

List of Photographs and Maps	i
Acknowledgments	iii
Introduction	1
Carroll's Brigade: Before Gettysburg	3
The March to Gettysburg	16
July 2: Morning Through Early Evening	32
Confederate Assault on East Cemetery Hill	50
Carroll's Brigade Arrives at Ricketts' Battery	82
Post-Battle Debate: 1864	96
The Debate is Renewed: 1876	109
General Howard Rekindles the Debate: 1885	112
"The Cannoneer" Adds Fuel to the Fire: 1889	120
Final Arguments: 1908	144
Epilogue	156
Appendix A:	
Selected Monuments and Markers on East Cemetery Hill	159
Appendix B:	
Order of Battle, Units Engaged on East Cemetery Hill, Evening, July 2, 1863	183
Bibliography	192
Index	201

LIST OF MAPS AND PHOTOGRAPHS

Colonel Nathan Kimball	4
The 7th West Virginia Infantry at Buffalo, West Virginia, 1862	6
Brigadier General William French	9
Surgeon Harry M. McAbee	10
Colonel John S. Mason	13
Colonel Samuel Sprigg Carroll	14
Map of Region Between Fredericksburg and Gettysburg	17
Brigadier General Alexander Hays	21
Elijah H. C. Cavins	26
Map of Gettysburg and the Surrounding Region	29
Major General Winfield Scott Hancock	30
Deployment of Carroll's Regiments, Morning, July 1	34
Colonel John Coons	36
Captain Peter Grubb	38
Lieutenant Colonel Franklin Sawyer	40
Lieutenant Colonel Leonard W. Carpenter	44
Path Taken to East Cemetery Hill by Carroll's Regiments	48
Lieutenant General Richard S. Ewell	51
Major General Jubal A. Early	53
Brigadier General Harry T. Hays	54
Colonel Isaac E. Avery	55
Brigadier General Adelbert Ames	57
Colonel Andrew L. Harris	58
View of Gettysburg	59
Colonel Leopold von Gilsa	60
Brigadier General Adolph von Steinwehr	62
Terrain Over Which Avery's North Carolinians Marched Toward East Cemetery Hill	64-65
Colonel Charles S. Wainwright	67
Stevens' 5th Maine Battery	68
Major Allen G. Brady	70
View of Stevens' Knoll and Culp's Hill	73
Major General Carl Schurz	75
Captain R. Bruce Ricketts	78
Second Lieutenant Charles F. Brockway	81
Map of Carroll's Arrival on East Cemetery Hill	84
Carroll's Men at Evergreen Cemetery Gatehouse	85

Evergreen Cemetery Gate	86
General Hays' Confederates Attacking Ricketts' Battery	88
Private John T. Whitzal	90
Major General Oliver Otis Howard	97
Brigadier General John Gibbon	101
Charles H. Myerhoff	115
Colonel Adin B. Underwood	117
Augustus Buell, "The Cannoneer"	121
William Houghton	123
Major Thomas W. Osborn	128
View of the 17th Connecticut Monument	135
View of Modern Day Wainwright Avenue	146-147
Location of Monuments and Markers on East Cemetery Hill	160
17th Connecticut Infantry Monument	161
14th Indiana Infantry Monument	163
14th Indiana Right Flank Marker	164
33rd Massachusetts Infantry Monument	165
41st New York Infantry Monument	166
54th New York Infantry Monument	167
68th New York Infantry Monument	168
134th New York Infantry Monument	169
Battery I, 1st New York Light Artillery Monument	170
4th Ohio Infantry Monument	171
4th Ohio Infantry Monument	172
25th and 75th Ohio Infantry Monument	173
25th and 75th Ohio Flank Markers	174
27th Pennsylvania Infantry Monument	175
73rd Pennsylvania Infantry Monument	176
106th Pennsylvania Infantry Marker	177
153rd Pennsylvania Infantry Marker	178
Battery B, 1st Pennsylvania Light Artillery Monument	180
Batteries F and G, 1st Pennsylvania Light Artillery Monument	181
7th West Virginia Infantry Monument	182

ACKNOWLEDGMENTS

Until Harry Pfanz's *Gettysburg: Culp's Hill and Cemetery Hill* was published, there had been woefully few serious treatments of the July 2, 1863 fighting on the Federal right flank. My contribution supplements Pfanz's exhaustive scholarship, as well as demonstrates how generally honorable men quarreled among themselves well after that sultry July evening for the honor of their respective units, and for history. Though short, this book benefited from the input of many people and institutions. To those who I have failed to mention, please accept my sincerest apologies.

Perhaps I should first acknowledge that group of Second and Eleventh Corps veterans and partisans who felt strongly enough about the role they and their respective units played on East Cemetery Hill, and how it should be remembered, to put their thoughts to paper.

I offer my sincere thanks to the following persons: Louise Arnold-French, Randy Hackenberg, Michael Winey, Dr. Richard Sommers and John Slonaker of the United States Army Military History Institute, Carlisle Barracks. Without knowing it, they were gracious, courteous and extremely helpful during my many visits to Carlisle. Their assistance made my job much easier. Mr. Dick Peterson of Gettysburg, Pennsylvania patiently listened to my pipe dream that became this book one November afternoon, and suggested that I make a serious attempt at publication. I am grateful to the staff of Reed Library, Fredonia State University College, particularly Ms. Margaret Pabst and her colleagues in the Interlibrary Loan Department, for tracking down many of the needed books. Deb Lanni's masterful photographic work was a godsend. I want to give a special thanks to Terry Lowry and David Richards for permission to use photographs from their collections.

I owe a special debt of gratitude to Jim McLean of Butternut and Blue for providing me the opportunity to have this work published. He also suggested that Dr. Richard Sauers edit the manuscript. Rick's thorough review forced me to rethink a few points which benefited the manuscript.

I am extremely grateful to the following institutions: Indiana Historical Society, Library of Congress, North Carolina Division of Archives and History, Bridgeport (Connecticut) Public Library and the National Archives.

The following organizations granted permission to quote from their collections/publications:

Simon and Schuster, Inc.: ***The Gettysburg Campaign***, Edwin B. Coddington.

The Kent State University Press: ***Fallen Leaves: The Civil War Letters of Major Henry Livermore Abbott***, Robert Garth Scott, editor; ***Connecticut Yankees at Gettysburg***, Charles P. Hamblin (Walter L. Powell, editor).

University of North Carolina Press: ***Gettysburg: Culp's Hill and Cemetery Hill***, Harry Pfanz.

New Hampshire Historical Society: original copies of the John B. Bachelder Papers.

I offer special thanks to two very good friends. Tim Shaw and I spent many hours walking the Gettysburg battlefield. Thanks for listening to me prattle on and on about what *may* have happened here and there. Al Poor, the quintessential Mainer, has helped me try to understand what the "Boys of '61" felt.

Finally, I would like to thank my wife, Eileen, and daughter, Jocelyn. Eileen, descendent from one of the Irish boys of the 69th Pennsylvania, accompanied me on many a battlefield trek in all types of weather and acted as a discerning sounding board. Her support, understanding and love far exceed my ability to thank her.

INTRODUCTION

As 1863 drew to a close, the men and officers of the Eleventh Corps of the Army of the Potomac, particularly its former First Division, found themselves the focus of ridicule and disdain. Many believed that troops of this division had performed in a cowardly manner against Confederate Lieutenant General Thomas Jonathan "Stonewall" Jackson's men at Chancellorsville. Then, two months later, on July 1, these same Federal troops, it was claimed, behaved in a similar fashion on the plains north of Gettysburg. Indeed, there was so much concern regarding the Eleventh Corps in general that only a few weeks after Gettysburg a number of its officers considered dismantling the corps and reassigning its various brigades and regiments to other commands.[1] As if this were not enough, in February 1864, General Howard and his men found themselves embroiled in a controversy regarding their alleged poor conduct in the fighting on East Cemetery Hill on the evening of July 2. This debate, which pitted Howard's First Division veterans against the Hoosiers, Buckeyes, and West Virginians of Colonel Samuel Sprigg Carroll's Second Corps brigade, swirled about the respective role that each of these units played in helping to defend threatened Federal artillery batteries on East Cemetery Hill. In the years after the war, the sometimes acerbic quarrel was carried out in a number of serial publications as well as in the pages of the leading Union-veteran newspaper, the *National Tribune*. Even today, histories that relate the fighting on July 2 may take very different views of the action on East Cemetery Hill.

Edwin Coddington, perhaps the foremost historian of the Gettysburg campaign and battle, wrote that although "the struggle for Cemetery Hill was one of the more dramatic and memorable events in the three days of bloody encounter between the two armies, its military

---

[1]United States War Department, *The War of the Rebellion: A Compilation of the Official Records of the Union and Confederate Armies*, 128 volumes (Washington, D.C.: Government Printing Office, 1880-1901), vol. 27, part 3, pp. 778-779, 785, 786 (hereinafter cited as *O.R. All references are to Series I, unless noted otherwise*).

importance has perhaps been overemphasized."[2] While this assessment may be close to the truth, one could never convince any of the Eleventh and Second Corps veterans, nor the artillerymen with whom they fought on that hazy evening in early July, that this action did not save the Union army from certain defeat at Gettysburg.

The first part of the story recounted here is that of Colonel Carroll's "Gibraltar Brigade," an uncommon unit composed of four western regiments in the eastern Federal army. After a grueling march north from near Fredericksburg, Virginia, Carroll's command arrived at the northern end of Cemetery Ridge early on the morning of July 2. That evening, three of the regiments rushed to the threatened Federal right flank where they encountered North Carolinians and Louisianians among the guns of Captain R. Bruce Ricketts' battery on East Cemetery Hill. Though their part in the fight lasted a very short time, these battle-tested veterans spent the next 50 years defending their sometimes overstated claim that they had been instrumental in helping to secure the Federal right. The story of this debate, the second part of the book, demonstrates how honorable men who were fighting for similar reasons saw and interpreted the same event in very different ways.

---

[2]Edwin B. Coddington, *The Gettysburg Campaign: A Study in Command* (New York: Charles Scribner's Sons, 1968), p. 438.

CARROLL'S BRIGADE: BEFORE GETTYSBURG

At the beginning of the summer of 1863, Colonel Samuel Sprigg Carroll's Second Brigade of the Second Division, Second Corps of the Army of the Potomac, was made up of battle-tested veterans from three western states. Indeed, such a brigade, composed of four western regiments (4th and 8th Ohio, 14th Indiana, and 7th West Virginia infantry regiments), was uncommon in the Army of the Potomac.[3]

Colonel Carroll's four regiments had been in service since the early days of the war. The 14th Indiana was organized at Terre Haute, Indiana, for a three-month term in May 1861. Less than one month later, however, the men reenlisted for three years' service, making the 14th the first three-years regiment provided by Indiana.[4] In early July, the Hoosiers left their home state fully armed and equipped for western Virginia. The regiment, commanded by Colonel Nathan Kimball, was initially assigned to Brigadier General William S. Rosecrans' Army of Occupation in western Virginia. The 14th spent much of the summer of 1861 on Cheat Mountain, Virginia where, on September 12, they first encountered General Robert E. Lee and his command in battle.[5]

The 4th Ohio was organized at Camp Jackson near Columbus, Ohio, two weeks after Fort Sumter surrendered. Shortly thereafter, the new recruits were sent to Camp Dennison near Cincinnati where they were mustered into three-months' service. Presently, the majority of the Buckeyes responded to President Abraham Lincoln's urgent call for more men by signing on for three-years' service. At the end of June, the regiment left Ohio for western Virginia where they were assigned to Colonel R.L. McCook's Advance Brigade of the Army of Occupation commanded at that time by Major General George B. McClellan. Roughly one month later the 4th was reassigned to the Third Brigade of

---

[3]The only other "western brigade" in the Army of the Potomac at the end of June 1863 was the renowned "Iron Brigade."

[4]Frederick H. Dyer, *Compendium of the War of the Rebellion*, 3 volumes (New York: Thomas Yoseloff, 1959), 3: 1124.

[5]"14th Indiana," *Rockwell Tribune*, September 12, 1889; Dyer, *Compendium of the War*, 1: 334.

Colonel Nathan Kimball

First commander of the 14th Indiana Infantry, Colonel Kimball later went on to command the "Gibraltar Brigade."

the Army of Occupation. After spending much of August and September skirmishing with the Confederates in the area around Cheat Mountain and Beverly, Virginia, the regiment was transferred to the Railroad District, Department of Western Virginia under command of Brigadier General B.F. Kelley. Under Kelley's leadership, the 4th helped clear Romney, Virginia of Confederate troops. The Buckeyes remained in that town until January 1862.[6]

The 8th Ohio was originally organized as a three-months regiment in the middle of April 1861. The citizen-soldiers gathered at Camp Dennison in a drenching rain where, "for the first time in their lives, [they] slept in the open air, with only a soldier's blanket for floor, roof, walls, and bedclothes." Responding to President Lincoln's call for 300,000 volunteers to squelch the rebellion, all of the original companies except one reenlisted for three-years' service. After leaving Ohio in July, the 8th was assigned to Brigadier General C.W. Hills' brigade of the Army of Occupation. Later that month the 8th joined the 4th Ohio in the Third Brigade in the Army of Occupation. During this time the Buckeyes were stationed at various locations along the Baltimore and Ohio Railroad. The men of the 8th Ohio in particular, suffered greatly from the effects of typhoid fever which they believed was contracted at a filthy bivouac site they named "Maggotty Hollow." In October, the 8th accompanied the 4th Ohio into the Railroad District of the Department of Western Virginia.[7]

The 7th West Virginia, formed in August 1861, was composed of Unionists from the towns of Portland, Cameron, Grafton, Wheeling, Morgantown and Greenland in western Virginia.[8] The Virginians did not

---

[6]*Ibid.*, pp. 334, 336; Whitelaw Reid, ***Ohio in the War; Her Statesmen, Her Generals, and Soldiers***, 2 volumes (Cincinnati, Ohio; Moore, Wilstach and Baldwin, 1868), 2: 36; In early September, three companies of the 4th Ohio-Companies A,F and K-were sent to southeastern Virginia where they were involved in minor skirmishing near Petersburg.

[7]*Ibid.*, 2: p. 66; Dyer, ***Compendium of the War***, 1: 334, 336.

[8]When mustered in, this regiment was known as the 7th Virginia Volunteers (for example, *O.R.*, vol. 12, part 3, pp. 4, 50). Herein, the 7th will be referred to as the 7th West Virginia, even in discussions pertaining to that period before West Virginia entered the Union.

**Image of the 7th West Virginia Infantry
at Buffalo, West Virginia, 1862.**

(*Terrance Lowry Collection, USAMHI.*)

get into the field until early in January 1862 when they joined the 4th and 8th Ohio in the Railroad District.[9]

The four regiments that would comprise Colonel Carroll's brigade at Gettysburg were finally consolidated in the same brigade in January 1862 when the 14th Indiana joined the 4th and 8th Ohio and 7th West Virginia. The brigade was commanded by the 14th Indiana's Col. Nathan Kimball and was officially designated as the First Brigade of Brigadier General F.W. Lander's division, Department of Western Virginia.[10] Early in March, Kimball's brigade was sent to Winchester, Virginia, where it prepared to set out after "Stonewall" Jackson's "foot cavalry." During April and May, the brigade moved up the Shenandoah Valley all the while skirmishing with Jackson's men at such locations as Woodstock, Mount Jackson, Edinburg, and New Market. Then, in the middle of May, Kimball's regiments were sent to Major General Irvin McDowell at Fredericksburg; within 24 hours, however, they were ordered back to Front Royal which had been overrun by Jackson's aggressive troops. At the end of June, Colonel Kimball's men finally left the valley for good. After arriving in Alexandria by rail, Kimball's regiments boarded transports for the trip to the Virginia Peninsula. The brigade arrived at Harrison's Landing on the James River on July 1 as the battle of Malvern Hill raged nearby.[11]

Brigadier General Kimball's command, recently redesignated "Kimball's Independent Brigade," was among the last to leave Harrison's Landing in August. It returned to Alexandria as Major General John Pope's Army of Virginia battled the Army of Northern Virginia to the west on the old Bull Run battlefield. Kimball's men were hurried toward the fighting and arrived in time to help cover the retreat of Pope's defeated army as it slogged back to the Washington defenses. Less than two weeks later the brigade was redesignated the First Brigade of Brigadier General

---

[9]Dyer, *Compendium of the War*, 3: 1663; T.F. Lang, *Loyal West Virginia from 1861 to 1865* (Baltimore, Maryland; The Deutsch Publishing Co., 1895), p. 265.

[10]At this time, Colonel Kimball's brigade also included the 84th Pennsylvania and 67th Ohio (Dyer, *Compendium of the War*, vol. 1: 336).

[11]"14th Indiana," *Rockwell Tribune*; Reid, *Ohio in the War*, 2: 37, 67; Lang, *Loyal West Virginia*, p. 265.

William H. French's Third Division of Major General Edwin V. "Bull" Sumner's Second Corps, Army of the Potomac.[12]

Late in the morning of September 17, Kimball's brigade, minus the 4th Ohio, was ordered to assault a sunken road east of Sharpsburg, Maryland.[13] The men stepped off toward the road and began ascending a ridge. Though it was somewhat fragmented by General French's two other brigades which had been repulsed from the road, Kimball's command continued forward in fine fashion. The four regiments were shaken by a number Confederate volleys as they crested the ridge in front of the sunken road but kept going forward. Kimball's men valiantly assaulted the right flank of Colonel John B. Gordon's Alabama brigade and the front of Brigadier General George B. Anderson's North Carolina brigade deployed in the sunken road. The Confederates in the road unleashed volley after volley, finally causing the Northerners to fall back. Kimball's First Brigade suffered the loss of 639 officers and men in front

---

[12]Reid, *Ohio in the War*, 2: pp. 37, 67; Dyer, *Compendium of the War*, 1: 294; Kimball was promoted to brigadier general on April 16, 1862 (Ezra Warner, *Generals in Blue* (Baton Rouge, Louisiana; Louisiana State University Press, 1964), p. 268.

[13]The 4th Ohio was apparently absent from the brigade at Antietam because of medical problems. On August 24, regimental surgeon H.M. McAbee wrote that of the 909 enlisted men in the regiment, only 300 were in good enough condition to be present for duty. McAbee attributed the poor health of the 4th to sickness acquired while at Harrison's Landing. As a result, army commander McClellan ordered the regiment into camp near Fort Gaines to recuperate. The 4th was replaced in Kimball's brigade by the 132nd Pennsylvania, a nine-months regiment. On September 19, McClellan ordered the Buckeyes to report for duty. This elicited a statement from the surgeon declaring that there were only 135 men fit for duty. Nine days later, those men deemed well boarded railroad cars for Harper's Ferry which they reached on the morning of the September 29 (William Kepler, *History of the Three Months and Three Years' Service of the Fourth Regiment Ohio Volunteer Infantry in the War for the Union* (Cleveland, Ohio; Leader Printing Co., 1886), pp. 81-83).

Brigadier General William French

In September 1862, Colonel Kimball's regiments were assigned to General French's Division, Second Corps, Army of the Potomac. One member of the 14th Indiana, E. H. C. Cavins, referred to French as "old whiskey tub."

Harry M. McAbee, Regimental Surgeon, 4th Ohio Infantry

(*USAMHI.*)

of the sunken road.[14] For its gallant behavior in the assault on the infamous "Bloody Lane," General Sumner labelled Kimball's command the "Gibraltar Brigade."[15]

Not long after Antietam, General Kimball's men found themselves involved in reconnaissance operations between Harper's Ferry and Leesburg, Virginia. At the end of October, the brigade broke camp and began marching toward the eastern part of Virginia. In the middle of November, the Gibraltar Brigade pulled up within several miles of Falmouth. Many of the men, anticipating the end of the campaigning season, began building winter quarters. This was premature for on December 12, Kimball's men were ordered to prepare to move. They, with the rest of General Sumner's Right Grand Division, were about to cross the Rappahannock River and enter Fredericksburg.[16]

The next morning, December 13, the 4th and 8th Ohio, along with the 1st Delaware, moved cautiously along the streets of Fredericksburg as skirmishers in advance of Kimball's brigade. The brigade, which now included two nine-months regiments, the 24th and 28th New Jersey, was part of General Sumner's force which would be thrown against Confederate infantry deployed in a sunken lane at the base of Marye's Heights. The Gibraltar Brigade moved out of the town, formed ranks and advanced at the double-quick through a rain of artillery and small arms fire toward the entrenched Southerners. Needless to say, they never reached the target; Kimball's men were pinned down in front of Marye's Heights. Late that afternoon, the brigade, lacking ammunition, was withdrawn into Fredericksburg. General Kimball was a severely wounded in the right leg during the fighting at the base of Marye's Heights and the brigade lost more than 500 men in this fruitless action. After recrossing the Rappahannock River, the "Gibraltar Brigade," now commanded by

---

[14]John M. Priest, *Antietam: The Soldiers' Battle* (Shippensburg, Pennsylvania: White Mane Publishing, Co., Inc., 1989), pp. 156-158, 336.

[15]Dyer, *Compendium of the War*, 1: 292; Lang, *Loyal West Virginia*, p. 267; Reid, *Ohio in the War*, 2: 68.

[16]Nancy Niblick Baxter, *Gallant Fourteenth. The Story of an Indiana Civil War Regiment* (Traverse City, Indiana: Pioneer Study Center Press, 1980), pp. 111, 113; Reid, *Ohio in the War*, 2: 37, 68; Kepler, *History of the Three Months*, p. 90.

Colonel John S. Mason of the 4th Ohio, went into winter quarters near Falmouth. With the exception of their participation in Major General Ambrose Burnside's ill-fated "mud march" in January, Mason's crippled regiments spent an uneventful winter trying to recuperate from Fredericksburg and prepare for the coming campaign.[17]

On April 28 the Gibraltar Brigade, including the two New Jersey regiments, ended its winter and early spring of inactivity. Early that morning the blueclad soldiers began marching northwest along the north bank of the Rappahannock River as part of Army of the Potomac commander Major General Joseph Hooker's well-conceived attempt to turn the left flank of the Army of Northern Virginia. They arrived at United States Ford that night and crossed the river on a pontoon bridge on the afternoon of April 30 as part of Major General William French's Third Division of the Second Corps, now commanded by Major General Darius N. Couch. The Gibraltar Brigade saw action in the scrubby pine growth north of Chancellorsville, losing more than 250 men in this fighting. Despite the promising start to this campaign, Hooker's men soon found themselves stumbling back to their old camps at Falmouth.[18]

At Chancellorsville, the Gibraltar Brigade was commanded by Colonel Samuel Sprigg Carroll, a 31-year old graduate of West Point. After graduating near the bottom of the class of 1856, Carroll had served on the western frontier and as quartermaster at West Point. Carroll, referred to as "Old Bricktop" by some of his men because of his flaming red hair, had been appointed colonel of the 8th Ohio in December 1861. The following spring he was elevated to brigade command in Brigadier General James Shields' division of the Department of the Rappahannock. In June 1862, Carroll took the reigns of a brigade in the Third Corps of General John Pope's Army of Virginia. Carroll was severely wounded while inspecting picket positions along the Rapidan River a short time

---

[17]Warner, *Generals in Blue*, pp. 268, 313; Dyer, *Compendium of the War*, 3: 1124, 1497, 1499, 1663; *O.R.*, vol. 25, part 2, pp. 532, 577; *Ibid.*, vol. 21, pp. 131, 291-293; Reid, *Ohio in the War*, 2: 37, 68; Lang, *Loyal West Virginia*, pp. 265-266.

[18]*O.R.*, vol. 25, part 1, p. 160, 364-365, 367; Reid, *Ohio in the War*, 2: 37, 68; Lang, *Loyal West Virginia*, p. 267; Ernest B. Furguson, *Chancellorsville 1863. The Souls of the Brave* (New York: Alfred A. Knopf, 1992), p. 353.

Colonel John S. Mason

Originally of the 4th Ohio, Colonel Mason assumed command of the "Gibraltar Brigade" after Colonel Carroll was wounded at Fredericksburg.

(Roger D. Hunt Collection, USAMHI.)

Colonel Samuel Sprigg Carroll

(*MOLLUS Collection, USAMHI.*)

before the battle of Second Bull Run. He recuperated in time to assume command of the Second Brigade of Brigadier General Amiel W. Whipple's Third Corps division at Fredericksburg. The following March, Carroll requested and was granted a transfer to the Second Corps. The colonel was assigned to command of the First Brigade, of the Second Division, Second Corps, Army of the Potomac.[19]

Colonel Carroll was known as a fighter. A member of George Meade's staff remembered the colonel as one of a group of men, which included Alexander Hays and George Custer, who "attacked wherever they got a chance, and of their own accord." Likewise, Eleventh Corps commander Major General Oliver O. Howard recalled that "For fearlessness and energetic action, Col. Carroll has not a superior." This is the reputation that Samuel Sprigg Carroll took with him to Gettysburg.[20]

---

[19] Warner, *Generals in Blue*, p. 73; Stewart Sifakis, ***Who Was Who in the Civil War*** (New York; Facts On File, Inc., 1988), p. 108; *O.R.*, vol. 21, p. 55; J.R. McClure, "Old Bricktop," *National Tribune*, December 5, 1889; Colonel Carroll appears to have gone on an extended sick leave in January 1862. While absent from the army, the regiments of his Third Corps brigade were transferred to various other commands. Division commander Whipple voiced concern over this in a dispatch dated March 9 to Brigadier General Seth Williams, Assistant Adjutant General, Army of the Potomac. Whipple worried that if Carroll were assigned to another brigade, the colonels of those regiments in the brigade may not take kindly to being commanded by an officer whose own regiment was in another brigade. This may explain why Carroll requested to be reassigned to the Second Corps. General Hooker responded by proposing that Carroll be reunited with the 8th Ohio (*Ibid.*, vol. 25, part 2, pp. 133-34).

[20] George R. Agassiz (editor), *Meade's Headquarters, 1863-1865, Letters of Colonel Theodore Lyman, From the Wilderness to Appomattox* (Boston, Massachusetts; Massachusetts Historical Society, 1922), p. 139; General O.O. Howard, letter, *Washington Daily Chronicle*, March 27, 1864.

THE MARCH TO GETTYSBURG

In early June, after satisfying himself that General Hooker was not about to move on Richmond, General Lee put his supremely confident Army of Northern Virginia on the road toward Culpeper Court House and the Shenandoah Valley beyond; Lee's second invasion of the North was underway. It soon became apparent that "Fighting Joe" Hooker's inactive army faced the prospect of being cut of from Washington. Jumping to action, Hooker quickly got his columns in motion headed north. The Second Corps would serve as the rear guard of the moving army.[21]

Colonel Carroll's men struck tents early on the morning of June 14 and prepared to march north with the rest of the Second Corps. Inevitable army delays, however, conspired to keep the brigade stationary until shortly after dark. The men spent an distressing night stumbling along dusty, rutted roads with only brief rests. The march north was continued early the next day, an "intensely hot" day which saw hundreds of men fall out of the struggling column. Sunstroke was particularly common and resulted in the deaths of a good number of men. It appears that all of the Second Corps ambulances were in action at the rear of the corps. All of this was made worse by pesky Confederate cavalry which nipped at the heels of the column.[22]

Colonel Carroll had the Gibraltar Brigade on the road before daylight on June 16, another oppressively hot and humid day. One of the toiling infantrymen recalled that "clouds of dust arose" from the marching column and "clothing and blankets were thrown away." Needless to say, straggling became a concern of those in command. Indeed, a member of the 8th Ohio recounted that during an afternoon halt in the march, an

---

[21]Coddington, *Gettysburg Campaign*, pp. 51, 75; Francis A. Walker, *History of the Second Army Corps in the Army of the Potomac* (New York; Charles Scribner's Sons, 1887), p. 258.

[22]Franklin Sawyer, *A Military History of the 8th Regiment Ohio Volunteer Infantry, Its Battles, Marches and Army Movements* (Cleveland, Ohio; Fairbanks, 1881), p. 119; Thomas Francis Galwey, *The Valiant Hours* (Harrisburg, Pennsylvania; The Stackpole Company, 1961), p. 90; Kepler, *History of the Three Months*, p. 119; Baxter, *Gallant Fourteenth*, p. 147; Walker, *Second Corps*, p. 258.

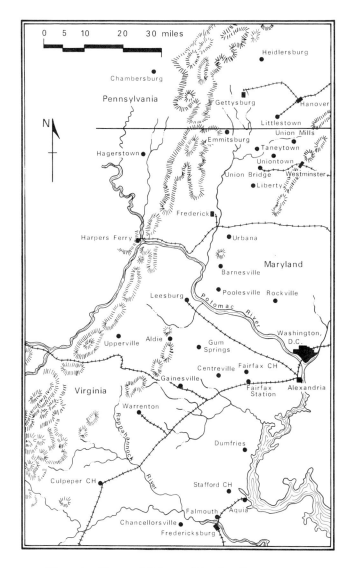

Map 1: General Map of Region Between Fredericksburg, Virginia and Gettysburg Pennsylvania

order was read declaring that "stragglers must be shot." Like the previous day, the flanks of the column continued to be harassed by Rebel "guerrillas" who were evidently bent on bagging the sick and straggling, as well as assorted horses and mules. Private William Kepler, future historian of the 4th Ohio, observed that some barns in the rear of the brigade had been torched. "It was currently reported," wrote Kepler, "that they were set on fire and the owners killed because they had bayoneted one of our men who was too sick to keep up with his command."[23]

By June 17, General Hooker had concentrated most of the Federal army in and around Centreville, Virginia, where the worn out men were given a few days to recover. Further relief came late the next day when a line of heavy thunderstorms passed through the area. In spite of this break in the heat wave, not everybody was enthralled with the rain. One of Colonel Carroll's men recalled that "one must either stand up or lie down in the mud; all night long somebody was stirring about, or growling about wet hips or leaky blankets." The pause in the march provided some of the more enterprising members of the 4th Ohio the opportunity to forage about the countryside "in spite of danger from the guerillas." A number of these men were able to lay in a nice supply of cherries and strawberries. While resting near Centreville, Carroll's troops heard rumors of a great cavalry battle fought to the west at a place called Brandy Station.[24]

During the short respite at Centreville, Colonel Carroll's brigade was diminished by one regiment. On June 19, the 28th New Jersey left for home, much "to the delight of the remainder of the brigade, who were getting tired of the continual talk about going home that some indulged in

---

[23]Kepler, *History of the Three Months*, p. 120; Galwey, *Valiant Hours*, p. 91.

[24]Kepler, *History of the Three Months*, p. 121.

whilst the country was in great danger."[25] The Gibraltar Brigade was now composed of the 4th and 8th Ohio, 14th Indiana and 7th West Virginia.[26]

Somewhat more refreshed but smaller in number, Carroll's brigade continued its trek north on Saturday June 20 in the van of the division column. The 8th Ohio was deployed as skirmishers to watch for any Rebels in the area. After marching a short time, the column crossed part of the Second Bull Run battlefield. The sights presented to the tough Second Corps veterans were ghastly. A year of rain had removed the thin layer of soil covering many of the dead of the previous two years. A Buckeye recalled that "unburied skeletons, bones and skulls lay scattered about the woods; sometimes half-buried remains extend their skeleton hands almost imploringly toward us." Private Lemuel Jefferies of Co. E, 4th Ohio, wrote in his diary that "on some of the skeletons clung part of the tattered blue uniform." A number of men of the 14th Indiana reported seeing evidence of mutilations and other atrocities performed on the bodies of the Union dead. In spite of the grisly spectacle revealed by the battlefield, one of Carroll's veterans declared that such "horrid sights are, to an older soldier, horrid no longer."[27]

Colonel Carroll's regiments reached Gainesville, where they would remain for several days, at about 6:00 p.m. on June 20. On June 24 the men learned that division commander French had been transferred to command of Federal forces at Harper's Ferry. Later that day, a general inspection was called and General French's farewell address was read to the gathered troops. Colonel Carroll was placed in command of the division until French's replacement, Brigadier General Alexander Hays,

---

[25]The 24th New Jersey had left Carroll's brigade on June 11, several days before the march north began. The 28th and 24th New Jersey regiments were mustered out of service on June 22 and 24, respectively (*Ibid.*, p. 119; *O.R.*, vol. 25, part 2, p. 532).

[26]Coddington, *Gettysburg Campaign*, p. 75; Kepler, *History of the Three Months*, p. 121; Sawyer, *A Military History of the 8th Regiment*, p. 119.

[27]Sawyer, *A Military History of the 8th Regiment*, pp. 119-120; Galwey, *Valiant Hours*, pp. 91-92; Kepler, *History of the Three Months*, p. 121; Jason H. Silverman (editor), "'The Excitement Had Begun!' The Civil War Diary of Lemuel Jefferies, 1862-1863," *Manuscripts*, vol. 30 (Fall 1978): 273-74; Baxter, *Gallant Fourteenth*, p. 148.

arrived. The following morning, the men of the Gibraltar Brigade packed their belongings and headed toward Gum Springs, all the while being shadowed by Confederate cavalry. Thomas Francis Galwey of the 8th Ohio groused that his regiment was ordered to serve as "wagon guard" during the march, "an extremely disagreeable task" characterized by periods of slow walking interrupted by bursts at the double-quick.[28]

By the morning of June 26, it had become obvious to many in the hierarchy of the Federal army that a part of the Army of Northern Virginia was on Pennsylvania soil. This knowledge heralded the beginning of a rapid push toward the Keystone State. Colonel Carroll's men marched past Leesburg and Ball's Bluff in a drizzling rain. They reached Edward's Ferry on the Potomac River at about 5:00 p.m. on the evening of the 26th and "took supper, [and] fixed ourselves down for the night." After finally falling asleep, the men "were routed out, fell into line, [and] waited for orders to march." They moved about a half-mile closer to the river and halted. Recalling the frustration of that night, Private Kepler of the 4th Ohio recorded that "some of us [were] getting out of sorts, some kept quiet, others blessed somebody, whilst everybody wondered, 'Why don't the Army of the Potomac move?'" After another hour or so of waiting, Kepler's wish was granted and the brigade crossed the Potomac on a pontoon bridge, finally setting foot on the Maryland shore at about 10:00 p.m. Circumstances on the north side of the river were not much better. Bringing up the rear of the army, Carroll's fatigued men plodded along roads that had been churned into what one soldier termed "mud soup." The wet and sullen infantrymen stumbled and slid about a mile from the river where they "collapsed in a muddy wheat field." In spite of the wretched conditions, most of the blueclad troops were in good spirits for, as one soldier proclaimed, "we were again in God's country."[29]

---

[28]Kepler, *History of the Three Months*, p. 122; *O.R.*, vol. 27, part 1, p. 142, 143; Galwey, *Valiant Hours*, pp. 93-95; Sawyer, *A Military History of the 8th Regiment*, p. 121; Baxter, *Gallant Fourteenth*, p. 148.

[29]Sawyer, *A Military History of the 8th Regiment*, pp. 121-122; Galwey, *Valiant Hours*, pp. 95-96. Kepler, *History of the Three Months*, pp. 122-123.

Brigadier General Alexander Hays

Commanded the Third Division of the Second Corps, Army of the Potomac.

(*MOLLUS Collection, USAMHI.*)

Colonel Carroll's men remained in their "muddy wheat field" until about 4:00 p.m. on June 27 when they took to the road again. After passing through Poolesville and Barnesville, Maryland, the four western regiments arrived at Sugar Loaf Mountain near midnight and bivouacked for what remained of the night. Early the next morning, the blue infantry fell into column and continued north. Late that afternoon the brigade pulled up at Monocacy Bridge several miles below Frederick, Maryland. Ironically, the Gibraltar Brigade bivouacked close to its camp site of September 13, 1862. No doubt the men recalled Antietam and wondered what this might portend for the near future.[30]

While at Monocacy Bridge some of the rank-and-file heard gossip that General Hooker had been replaced as army chief by Fifth Corps commander Major General George Gordon Meade. Ohioan Thomas Galwey believed that the change in command might be good for the army insomuch as many senior officers had apparently lost confidence in Hooker after Chancellorsville. While considering the latest change in army command, Lieutenant Galwey expressed a desire no doubt shared by many of his comrades in arms; that General in Chief Major General Henry W. Halleck and Secretary of War Edwin M. Stanton might be captured by Confederate General "Jeb" Stuart's cavalry rumored to be headed for Washington.[31]

The men of the Gibraltar Brigade made the most of their short stay at Monocacy Bridge. Supply wagons, which had trailed the column, finally caught up to the brigade and the soldiers were issued much needed clothes. Additionally, many of the grimy troops "wearing" the soil of the roads over which they had marched, took this opportunity to bathe in Monocacy Creek. Some men foraged locally and a number of "thirsty" Yankees stole into Frederick in search of liquor. Colonel Carroll, who had recently been sick, rejoined his brigade at Monocacy Bridge. During his absence, the brigade had been commanded by Colonel John Coons of the 14th Indiana.[32]

---

[30]Walker, *History of the Second Corps*, p. 261; Sawyer, *A Military History of the 8th Regiment*, p. 122; Galwey, *Valiant Hours*, p. 96; Kepler, *History of the Three Months*, p. 123.

[31]Galwey, *Valiant Hours*, p. 96.

[32]Kepler, *History of the Three Months*, p. 123; Sawyer, *A Military History of the 8th Regiment*, p. 122; Baxter, *Gallant Fourteenth*, p. 148.

Armed with a better understanding of the urgent situation facing the Army of the Potomac than his predecessor, on June 28 General Meade issued challenging marching orders to be carried out the next day. Carroll's men were ready to go before the sun came up on June 29. Unfortunately they did not move until that afternoon, the hottest time of a scorching day.[33] After finally getting underway, Carroll's bluecoats marched continuously "with scarcely a halt for dinner, and none for supper." The stifling weather, road dust and pace of the march combined to induce a great deal of straggling during the evening and night. Although 8th Ohio member Thomas Galwey considered himself a good marcher, he was overcome by exhaustion near dark and forced to fall out of the laboring column. A rainstorm awoke the sleeping Galwey and he began limping after his regiment. While on the road the Buckeye came upon an acquaintance from New York and, agreeing that they were "played out," both men retired to a nearby barn for the night.[34]

The rain that woke Lieutenant Galwey made fording small streams and creeks along the route of march difficult at best. Nonetheless, the act of fording the swollen streams slowed the pace of the march affording the men a modicum of rest. Colonel Carroll's men suffered more than other members of the Second Corps because of their position at the rear of the brigade wagon train. The roads had been trounced into a sea of mud making the marching that much more strenuous. Lieutenant Colonel Franklin Sawyer, commanding officer and future historian of the

---

[33]Franklin Sawyer, *The Eighth Ohio at Gettysburg. Address by General Franklin Sawyer* (Washington, D.C.: Regimental Association, E.J. Gray, Printer, 1889), p. 3; Galwey, *Valiant Hours*, p. 96; Sawyer, *A Military History of the 8th Regiment*, p. 122; At 7:00 a.m. on June 29, Second Corps commander Major General Winfield Scott Hancock informed General Meade's chief of staff, Major General Daniel Butterfield, that the Second Corps march had been delayed three hours because a corps clerk failed to deliver the orders from army headquarters. Hancock added that his men were about to take to the road. Somewhat later, Seth Williams, responding for Meade, suggested that the person responsible for the oversight be punished. The Second Corps commander wrote back that the "man in question has already been brought to punishment." Hancock went on to state that he would make up for the delay by taking "short cuts and rapid marching" (*O.R.*, vol. 27, part 3, pp. 395-396).

[34]Galwey, *Valiant Hours*, p. 97; Private Galwey caught up to his regiment the next morning.

8th Ohio, recalled that his men had become so jaded that many of them fell "asleep as they rested on their muskets [for] a moment." The weary column came to a thankful halt several miles south of Uniontown, Maryland between 2:00 and 3:00 a.m. on June 30. They had marched between 30 and 35 miles in roughly 12 hours, passing through Frederick, Liberty, Jamestown and Union Bridge, Maryland.[35]

Later in the morning of June 30, the Gibraltar Brigade tramped about one mile to Uniontown where they were united with the major part of the Second Corps. The men collapsed out of the column; some simply fell asleep in place while others took advantage of the "cordial and inspiring" welcome offered by the people of Uniontown. The tired Northerners were provided refreshments by the Unionists of the town and "kind words and good cheer lifted the hearts of the weary soldiers." That afternoon, roll was called and the men were mustered for pay. On this day, Colonel Carroll's four regiments totaled 1081 men and officers.[36]

Colonel Carroll's men were up early on Wednesday July 1 and on the road by 7:00 a.m. Marching at a leisurely pace, they reached Taneytown, Maryland, at about 9:30 a.m.[37] Near noon the men were ordered to proceed north to the small village of Gettysburg, Pennsylvania. The bluecoats fell into column and began marching, little understanding the gravity of this order. After a short time, these veterans of many other fields heard the unmistakable sounds of artillery reverberating from the

---

[35]Sawyer, *The Eighth Ohio at Gettysburg*, p. 3; Sawyer, *A Military History of the 8th Regiment*, p. 122; Kepler, *History of the Three Months*, p. 123; Galwey, *Valiant Hours*, p. 98.

[36]Sawyer, *A Military History of the 8th Regiment*, p. 122; Galwey, *Valiant Hours*, p. 98; Kepler, *History of the Three Months*, p. 123; Walker, *History of the Second Corps*, p. 262; The strengths of Colonel Carroll's four regiments on June 30 were as follows: 14th Indiana⇒229; 4th Ohio⇒292; 8th Ohio⇒272; 7th West Virginia⇒281. These size of each of these regiments was less than the average size (308 men) of a Federal regiment at Gettysburg (John W. Busey and David G. Martin, *Regimental Strengths and Losses at Gettysburg* (Hightstown, New Jersey: Longstreet House, 1986) pp. 42, 229.

[37]Galwey, *Valiant Hours*, p. 98; General Hancock had ordered the Second Corps to Taneytown earlier that morning (*O.R.*, vol. 27, part 1, p. 367).

north and warning of "a severe battle in that direction." The racket generated by the artillery was attended by "grim clouds of dust and smoke that gathered gloomily along the otherwise clear sky away to our front." Though the swelling volume of the artillery duel to the north hastened the men toward Gettysburg, Lieutenant Colonel Elijah H.C. Cavins of the 14th Indiana wrote in his diary that the men enjoyed "a leisurely march over a high-cultivated country."[38]

After marching roughly four miles from Taneytown, the column was halted and General Orders 67 was read to the men. This brief statement, dated June 28, made it official; General Meade was in command of the Army of the Potomac.

> By direction of the President of the United States, I hereby assume command of the Army of the Potomac. As a soldier, in obeying this order-an order totally unexpected and unsolicited-I have no promises or pledges to make. The country looks to this army to relieve it from the devastation and disgrace of a hostile invasion. Whatever fatigues and sacrifices we may be called upon to undergo, let us have in view constantly the magnitude of the interests involved, and let each man determine to do his duty, leaving to an all-controlling Providence the decision of the contest. It is with just diffidence that I relieve in the command of this army an eminent and accomplished soldier, whose name must ever appear conspicuous in the history of its achievements; but I rely

---

[38]Sawyer, *The Eighth Ohio at Gettysburg*, p. 3; Sawyer, *A Military History of the 8th Regiment*, p. 123; Galwey, *Valiant Hours*, p. 98; David E. Beem, Gettysburg Speech, 1887, United States Army Military History Institute, Carlisle Barracks, Carlisle, Pennsylvania; E.H.C. Caines, "A Gettysburg Diary, Carroll's Brigade and the Part It Played in Repulsing the Tigers," *National Tribune*, December 23. 1909; The surname "Caines" appears to have been a misprint. The Hoosier wrote a letter to John Bachelder in May 1878 and signed it "Cavins." Herein, Caines will be referred to by what appears to be his correct name, Elijah H.C. Cavins (Elijah H.C. Cavins to John Bachelder, May 9, 1878, *in* David L. Ladd and Audrey J. Ladd (editors), *The Bachelder Papers. Gettysburg in Their Own Words* 3 volumes (Dayton, Ohio: Press of the Morningside Bookshop, 1994-95), 1: 558.

**Post-War Image of Elijah H. C. Cavins
of the 14th Indiana Infantry**

upon the hearty support of my companions in arms to
assist me in the discharge of the duties of the important
trust which has been confided to me.

This finished, Colonel Carroll simply instructed his troops to, "Do as you have always done." General Orders 67 appears to have influenced the men in different ways. Whereas one soldier believed that the order had a "good effect upon everyone," another man opined that it was too tame and should have stressed the destruction of Lee's army. Regardless, the march continued northward at a brisk pace.[39]

The column had not been marching long before the men began hearing gossip of fierce fighting north and west of Gettysburg and, more than that, the Federal troops already on the field were getting the worst of it. This news appears to have impelled the bluecoats forward with even greater resolve and determination. Private Kepler proudly proclaimed that "there was no straggling...no urging to 'close up;' the ripening cherries and apples, and abundance of forage, enticed but few from their places."[40] Near 5:00 p.m., the van of Colonel Carroll's column encountered an ambulance bearing the body of Major General John Reynolds. The men of the western brigade reacted with profound silence and one Buckeye remarked that there were "no more jokes."[41]

Rumors that "the gallant First Corps was cut to pieces and that it and the Eleventh Corps were in full retreat" continued to ripple along the marching column. This lamentable news was made painfully evident by the flotsam and jetsam of the fighting to the north encountered all along the road. Indeed, at times the column was hindered by fleeing soldiers and ambulances that filled the road. John Galwey recalled seeing refugees from the fighting

> gathered in little crowds about their fires, boiling coffee
> and babbling German. All talking at once; without

---

[39] Galwey, *Valiant Hours*, p. 98; Kepler, *History of the Three Months*, pp. 123-124; *O.R.*, vol. 27, part 3, p. 374.

[40] Caines, "A Gettysburg Diary"; Sawyer, *The Eighth Ohio at Gettysburg*, p. 3; David Beem, Speech, USAMHI; Kepler, *History of the Three Months*, p. 123.

[41] Sawyer, *A Military History of the 8th Regiment*, p. 123; Kepler, *History of the Three Months*, p. 123; Baxter, *Gallant Fourteenth*, p. 149.

officers, without organization of any sort; a mere herd of stragglers. During the night, however, the provost guards drove them ignominiously forward to their positions.[42]

Around dark, Colonel Carroll, at the head of his column which was now within two or three miles of Gettysburg, met Major General Hancock who was riding from the battlefield to General Meade's headquarters at Taneytown. Carroll stopped to chat with his superior about the fighting in and around Gettysburg as well as the position that Hancock had selected to defend. As he rode off, Carroll turned in his saddle and asked Hancock if the position was a good one. "If Lee does not attack before all our forces are up," Hancock proclaimed, "we can hold the position I have selected against the whole Confederacy."[43]

Before he continued on his way to Taneytown, Hancock advised Carroll that his troops could rest for the night. The corps commander cautioned, however, that the men should be ready to move forward and take position early the next morning. Carroll's footsore infantrymen filed into a meadow "near the foot of two mountain spurs [probably the Round Tops], and stacked arms." A member of the 4th Ohio fondly remembered the evening as "balmy and beautiful, though somewhat hazy, but with sufficient moonlight." The quietude of the night periodically was interrupted by "the lumbering roll of artillery moving up to available positions for the morning and the loud shouts of men losing one another in the dark, in their search for their everlasting coffee." Later that night, according to Buckeye Thomas Galwey, Carroll's men were ordered to move forward to the area near Power's Hill, somewhat less than one mile in the rear of Cemetery Ridge. After stumbling through the dark, the Gibraltar Brigade reached its destination at about 3:00 a.m. on July 2.

---

[42]David Beem, Speech, USAMHI; Galwey, *Valiant Hours*, p. 100.

[43]Caines, "A Gettysburg Diary"; Sawyer, *A Military History of the 8th Regiment*, p. 123; Sawyer, *The Eighth Ohio at Gettysburg*, p. 3; Kepler, *History of the Three Months*, p. 124; At about 7:00 p.m. on the evening of July 1, General Hancock turned command of the field over the Major General Henry W. Slocum, the highest ranking Federal officer at Gettysburg at that time. Hancock then rode back to Taneytown to report to General Meade (*O.R*, vol. 27, part 3, pp. 368-369, 704).

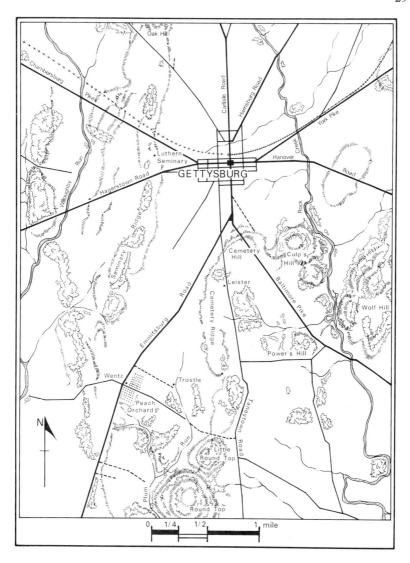

Map 2: General Map of Gettysburg and Surrounding Region

Major General Winfield Scott Hancock

Commanded the Second Corps, Army of the Potomac. It was at his request that Colonel Carroll's three regiments would be sent toward the sound of fighting on East Cemetery Hill on the evening of July 2, 1863.

(*MOLLUS Collection, USAMHI.*)

The bluecoats fell out of column and, for the few remaining hours left of the night, slept on their arms.[44]

---

[44]Galwey, *Valiant Hours*, p. 100; Silverman, "The Excitement Had Begun," p. 274; Sawyer, *The Eighth Ohio at Gettysburg*, p. 3; Kepler, *History of the Three Months*, p. 124; Sawyer, *A Military History of the 8th Regiment*, p. 123; "F," "Gettysburg. A Spirited Account of the Battle, and the Part Taken Therein by the 8th Ohio," *National Tribune*, August 20, 1885.

JULY 2: MORNING THROUGH EARLY EVENING

Colonel Carroll's troops were up at about 4:00 a.m. on Thursday, July 2. One man recalled hearing artillery fire from both sides even at that early hour.[45] Some of the men were able to wash up and scratch together a quick breakfast; others had to eat their hardtack and salt pork on the road. Somewhat before the sun came up, Carroll's men fell in and began marching toward Gettysburg on the Baltimore Pike.[46]

The column had travelled only a short distance when it halted for about one hour. Evidently believing that serious work lay ahead, a number of Carroll's men spent some time "furbishing up their arms [and] getting their cap and cartridge boxes in shape." Up and on the road again, the Gibraltar Brigade finally arrived in their assigned position at the northern end of Cemetery Ridge at about 8:00 a.m. Division commander Alexander Hays ordered Carroll to form his brigade *en masse* just to the east of the Brian farm buildings. The four regiments massed to the right and rear of Lieutenant George A. Woodruff's six 12-pounders of Battery I, 1st United States Artillery and within Ziegler's Grove.[47] Carroll's four

---

[45]Galwey, *Valiant Hours*, p. 101; J.L. Dickelman, "Gen. Carroll's Gibraltar Brigade at Gettysburg, Fighting on Different Parts of the Line," *National Tribune*, December 10, 1908; Sawyer, *The Eighth Ohio at Gettysburg*, p. 3; William Kepler of the 4th Ohio believed that the men were awaken at 3:00 a.m. That was approximately the time that the brigade reached Cemetery Hill and is probably too early (Kepler, *History of the Three Months*, p. 126).

[46]David Beem, Speech, USAMHI; Sawyer, *The Eighth Ohio at Gettysburg*, p. 3; Galwey, *Valiant Hours*, p. 101; Kepler, *History of the Three Months*, p. 126; Silverman, "The Excitement Had Begun," p. 274; Sawyer, *A Military History of the 8th Regiment*, p. 123.

[47]Sawyer, *A Military History of the 8th Regiment*, p. 123; Galwey, *Valiant Hours*, p. 101; Caines, "A Gettysburg Diary"; Sawyer, *The Eighth Ohio at Gettysburg*, p. 4; The exact location and deployment of Colonel Carroll's brigade at the north end of Cemetery Ridge appears to have changed during the morning of July 2. Lieutenant Colonel Jonathan Lockwood of the 7th West Virginia simply reported that the brigade was "massed in front of the enemy." Colonel Carroll wrote that his command was formed in line of regiments and Colonel Coons of the 14th Indiana recorded that Woodruff's battery was located

regiments held the right flank of the Second Corps and connected with the left of the Eleventh Corps on the Taneytown Road. From their position at the northern end of Cemetery Ridge, the colonel's veterans gazed to the west across the valley toward Seminary Ridge where they could see "the bare outline of the rebel works and army."[48]

A number of Colonel Carroll's men recounted that the field was shrouded in "comparative quiet" with "no considerable firing." Lemuel Jefferies of the 4th Ohio scrawled in his diary that "comparative quiet reigned along the front of both lines for several hours."[49] Others remembered things quite differently. General Hancock, for example, wrote that "sharp skirmishing occurred at intervals during the morning" and Thomas Galwey claimed that at times, very intense skirmish activity raged in the low valley between Cemetery and Seminary ridges. A member of the 14th Indiana wrote in his diary that "a lively skirmish has been kept up all morning, with an occasional artillery shot from our guns."

---

near the center of the brigade line. Another member of the 14th recalled that the right of his regiment rested in Ziegler's Grove and supported Woodruff's battery. The historian of the 4th Ohio maintained that "the brigade was formed in line of regiments." Almost 20 years after the battle Thomas Galwey recalled that at some point during the morning the brigade was in line along a stone fence that extended from the Taneytown Road toward Zeigler's Grove. Galwey claimed that the 8th Ohio held the right of the line with its right flank resting on the road. John Bachelder's map of the troop positions for July 2, 1863 shows the three brigades of General Hays' division massed in column of regiments by brigades. It is likely that Carroll's regiments moved from a massed grouping into line later in the morning (*O.R.*, vol. 27, part 1, pp. 456, 458, 463, ;"M," "Gettysburg. What the 14th Ind. Did in the Fight," *National Tribune*, September 10, 1885; Kepler, *History of the Three Months*, p. 126; Thomas F. Galwey to John B. Bachelder, May 19, 1882, *in* Ladd and Ladd, *Bachelder Papers*, 2: 868; Positions of Troops (map), Second Day's Battle, *in Ibid.*)

[48]*O.R.*, vol. 27, part 1, p. 369; Sawyer, *The Eighth Ohio at Gettysburg*, p. 4.

[49]Sawyer, *The Eighth Ohio at Gettysburg*, pp. 3-4; Sawyer, *A Military History of the 8th Regiment*, p. 125; Silverman, "The Excitement Had Begun," p. 274.

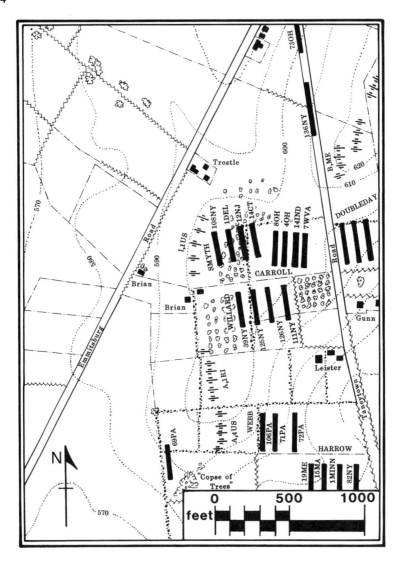

Map 3: Deployment of Colonel Carroll's Regiments and Other Units, Morning, July 1

Similarly, Colonel John Coons, commander of the 14th, recalled that "a lively skirmish was kept up all morning."[50]

Between 9:00 and 9:30 a.m. General Hays, probably in response to persistent skirmish activity on his front, ordered Colonel Carroll to deploy four companies of the 4th Ohio in support of the 1st Delaware already west of the Emmitsburg Road in the vicinity of the Bliss Farm. The Ohioans hurried down the west flank of the ridge to the road from where they "kept up a brisk interchange of shots with the enemy's skirmishers."[51]

In spite of the skirmishing on their front, many of Carroll's men were able to find diversions to occupy their time. Lieutenant Colonel Sawyer of the 8th Ohio recalled that many of the blueclad soldiers were able to rest in spite of "the gloomy ambulances rattling along [the Taneytown Road] with their moaning occupants." A private in the 4th Ohio observed "large detachments of troops...in motion, artillery getting into position, and ammunition trains; also the gloomy ambulances hurrying along with full loads of groaning wounded." Some men penned letters to friends and loved ones at home while others scribbled in their diaries. Many soldiers simply stretched out behind the stone fences that traversed the north end of Cemetery Ridge and talked among themselves or slept. Those veterans of two years of hard fighting who understood what lay ahead "fixed up their guns-put their cap and cartridge boxes in shape and in other ways prepared for the conflict they knew was coming."[52]

---

[50]Caines, "A Gettysburg Diary"; *O.R.*, vol. 27, part 1, pp. 369, 458; Galwey, *Valiant Hours*, p. 102.

[51]*O.R.*, vol. 27, part 1, pp. 456-457, 460; Elwood Christ, *"Over a Wide, Hot,...Crimson Plain"-The Struggle for the Bliss Farm at Gettysburg* (Baltimore: Butternut and Blue, 1993), p. 19.

[52]Sawyer, *A Military History of the 8th Regiment*, p. 125; Silverman, Jefferies diary, p. 274; Sawyer, *The Eighth Ohio at Gettysburg*, p. 4; William Kepler recalled that "the men soon busied themselves getting their arms in the best possible order [and] blankets and cartridge-boxes into comfortable position" (Kepler, *History of the Three Months*, p. 126).

Colonel John Coons

Commanded the 14th Indiana Infantry at Gettysburg.

(*Indiana Historical Society.*)

Buckeye infantryman William Kepler recalled that although some men were able to content themselves by sleeping or writing, the more inquisitive wandered a short distance toward the front "to get a better view of what was happening." One of these men, George Washington Lambert of the 14th Indiana, was watching Colonel Carroll sitting his horse when a minie ball passed dangerously close to the officer's head. The Hoosier recalled that Carroll turned and remarked to a member of his staff with a laugh, "Did you see that damned rascal shoot at me?"[53]

Skirmish fire at the northern end of Cemetery Ridge began to dwindle around noon, permitting some officers, their aides, and other men to become "quite bold taking observations" of the Confederate lines across the valley. Between 1:00 and 2:00 p.m., however, Southern batteries, probably directing their fire against Woodruff's guns, began dropping shells among Colonel Carroll's men. In addition to scattering Yankees on the ridge, the artillery fusillade provided cover to Rebel pickets who began to work toward the Emmitsburg Road.[54] Fully cognizant of the perilous situation on his front, Carroll ordered Companies G and I of the 4th Ohio under command of Captain Peter Grubb to relieve the four Buckeye companies already on the skirmish line. The Ohioans pressed the Confederates on their front and then formed a line near the Emmitsburg Road to the left of what was probably the Brian tenant buildings at the end of the Brian farm lane, where they erected a barricade of fence rails.[55]

In spite of their early success, Captain Grubb's two companies as well as the other skirmish units along and to the west of the Emmitsburg Road were in a quandary. Confederate skirmishers and sharpshooters began to move into the natural rifle pit formed where the road transected a slight elevation at the north end of Cemetery Ridge. Southern riflemen in

---

[53]*Ibid.*, p. 127; Baxter, ***Gallant Fourteenth***, p. 150.

[54]Kepler, ***History of the Three Months***, p. 127; ***O.R.***, vol. 27, part 1, p. 457; Sawyer, ***Valiant Hours***, p. 125; Colonel Carroll reported that the Confederates fired between 12 and 24 artillery rounds at his position.

[55]***O.R.***, vol. 27, part 1, pp. 457, 460; Kepler, ***History of the Three Months***, pp. 126-127; Colonel Carroll recorded that Companies G and I were deployed at about noon; Lieutenant Colonel Leonard Carpenter of the 4th Ohio believed that the two companies were ordered forward at about 3:00 in the afternoon (***O.R.***, vol. 27, part 1, pp. 457, 460).

Captain Peter Grubb, 4th Ohio Infantry

the road began picking off orderlies, officers, and artillerymen on the ridge. General Hays, alerted to the threat on his front, ordered Colonel Carroll to clear and hold the rifle pit that was the Emmitsburg Road. It was about 4:00 p.m. and the fighting on Major General Daniel E. Sickles' advanced front to the south had started. Carroll, however, had more immediate problems on his front and ordered Lieutenant Colonel Franklin Sawyer to prepare to send the entire 8th Ohio against the Southerners sheltered along the Emmitsburg Road.[56]

Franklin Sawyer faced a daunting task. His men would have to cross almost 200 yards of open ground. Resigned to their fate, the Buckeyes prepared for the assault by capping their rifles and fixing bayonets. Sawyer pointed out the position he had been assigned to take and mounted his horse. The colonel jumped his horse over the stone fence; he was followed by his men who quickly reformed into line of battle. Sawyer then ordered the men to "double quick" down the slope toward the Emmitsburg Road which they did with a shout. John Galwey crowed that the regiment "moved down the hill in line of battle in fine style, our colors flying." As the Ohioans ran toward the sunken length of the Emmitsburg Road, they were cheered on by the balance of the brigade as well as artillerymen of Captain James A. Hall's Battery B, 2nd Maine Light Artillery "posted on the left of the cemetery." Some of the latter had climbed on their guns and were waving flags, handerkerchiefs, hats and swords.[57]

The Confederates along the road began pouring a stinging fire into the Ohioans running toward them. Sawyer recalled that "the balls came thick and spitefully among us, the men began to fall, some killed,

---

[56]Sawyer, *The Eighth Ohio at Gettysburg*, p. 4; Sawyer, *A Military History of the 8th Regiment*, p. 126; "F," "A Spirited Account of the Battle"; *O.R.*, vol. 27, part 1, p. 457; Lieutenant Colonel Sawyer wrote that he had originally been directed by Carroll to send four companies as an advanced picket line which was to be supported by the remainder of the regiment and that he was ordered "to hold my line to the last man" (*O.R.*, vol. 27, part 1, p. 461).

[57]Christ, *"Over a Wide, Hot,...Crimson Plain,"* p. 33; Sawyer, *A Military History of the 8th Regiment*, p. 126; "F," "A Spirited Account of the Battle"; Galwey, *Valiant Hours*, p. 103; Sawyer, *The Eighth Ohio at Gettysburg*, p. 4; *O.R.*, vol. 27, part 1, p. 360; Because the 8th Ohio's line had been facing north at this time, the Buckeyes probably moved by the left flank down the slope.

Lieutenant Colonel Franklin Sawyer

Commanded the 8th Ohio Infantry of Colonel Carroll's brigade at Gettysburg. Sawyer's regiment did not accompany its sister regiments to East Cemetery Hill, but rather remained in the fields just west of the Emmitsburg Pike where they faced Confederates deployed in and around the Bliss Farm.

(*MOLLUS Collection, USAMHI.*)

some wounded, but we swept until we came to the" Emmitsburg Road. Sensing that the tables were turning, the Rebels struggled to get out of the road that was bounded on both sides by high post-and-rail fences. Most of them soon realized that their only avenue of escape was down the road. Sawyer's men fired at some of the fleeing Confederates, killing several of them. Although many of the Southerners were able to elude the bluecoats, 50 to 70 were captured by the plucky Buckeyes.[58]

Their ardor up, many of Lieutenant Colonel Sawyer's men continued beyond the Emmitsburg Road all the way to a fenceline in the fields west of the road. Sawyer quickly ordered that the fence be taken down "and the rails piled along so as to improve the hight [sic] of his 'rifle-pit'" along the road. The officer then deployed Companies A and I under command of Captain Azor H. Nickerson, as an advanced skirmish line "into the corn" well west of the Emmitsburg Road. The remainder of the regiment was withdrawn to the strengthened rifle pit along the road near the unoccupied Brian tenant farm house which served as a temporary aid station. In short order, some of the Ohioans climbed to the second floor of the building and began firing through holes they had punched in the roof. The 8th Ohio suffered the loss of one man killed and 13 wounded in this action.[59]

It was probably not until shortly after 5:00 p.m. that Lieutenant Colonel Sawyer had finally deployed the 8th Ohio along and to the west of the Emmitsburg Road. By this time General James Longstreet's attack on Sickles' Third Corps was well underway. One of Sawyer's men recalled that "Sickles's great battle was being fought with desperation to our left, and much of the terrific struggle could plainly be observed from our position." Roughly 30 minutes later Colonel George L. Willard's brigade of General Hays' division was ordered to move by the left flank to a position almost one mile to the south. This left only Colonel Carroll's and Colonel Thomas A. Smyth's brigades at the north end of Cemetery Ridge.

---

[58]Sawyer, *A Military History of the 8th Regiment*, p. 126; Sawyer, *The Eighth Ohio at Gettysburg*, p. 4; Galwey, *Valiant Hours*, p. 103; "F," "A Spirited Account of the Battle."

[59]Sawyer, *A Military History of the 8th Regiment*, pp. 126-127; Galwey, *Valiant Hours*, p. 103; "F," "A Spirited Account of the Battle"; Sawyer, *The Eighth Ohio at Gettysburg*, p. 4; "F" reported that two men had been killed and 13 wounded.

Perhaps 30 minutes after Willard departed for the south part of the field, Confederate artillery across the valley opened a "heavy and continuous" bombardment of Carroll's and Smyth's men and Lieutenant Woodruff's battery.[60] Recalling the onset of the fusillade, William Kepler of the 4th Ohio wrote:

> before 6 o'clock the firing on the left was more rapid, accompanied by the whirr of musketry, while troops could be soon hurrying forward over the plain from our side; in a few minutes more there was unusual activity among the spectres in the shadow of the trees on our front, then a puff of smoke, a shot went over our heads, then another, and a third scattered a stack of guns of the rear regiment, the Seventh Virginia, plunging a bayonet into a comrade's side and another cut a comrade of the Fourth in twain; now there was hurrying to and fro, men for their companies and their guns...a solid shot plowed through an orderly's horse....The batteries in front of us were now replying vigorously....whizzing shot and whirring shell, plunging and ricocheting among and over us for more than an hour, were making our position uncomfortable....The direful roar of cannon was added[,] the whirr of musketry, hissing minies, shrieking shell and screaming shot, whilst the air was darkening with clouds of sulphurous smoke, obscuring the hiding sun."[61]

The Confederate bombardment had the bluecoats scrambling for cover. Elijah Cavins of the 14th Indiana recalled a 12-pound shell falling next to him. David Beem, commanding officer of Company H, 14th Indiana, wrote that "in all my experience heretofore I was never under such terrible shelling." In spite of all that was going on around him, Beem was able to observe the furious fighting engulfing the southern end of Cemetery Ridge. After all was said and done, the Confederate artillery

---

[60]Christ, *"Over a Wide, Hot,...Crimson Plain,"* p. 42; "F," "A Spirited Account of the Battle"; Harry W. Pfanz, *Gettysburg-The Second Day* (Chapel Hill, North Carolina: The University of North Carolina Press, 1987), p. 405; *O.R.*, vol. 27, part 1, p. 457.

[61]Kepler, *History of the Three Months*, p. 127.

barrage did much less damage than would have been thought based on its intensity. Indeed, a member of the 14th Indiana recalled that although "the whistling of solid shot and shell about us was simply terrific...the wonder was that our loss was so small."[62]

At about 6:00 p.m. or shortly thereafter, General Hays ordered Colonel Carroll to move his three remaining regiments—the 14th Indiana, 4th Ohio (minus Companies G and I), and 7th West Virginia—"by the left flank, and take position on the left of the Second Brigade [Colonel Smyth's brigade]." This change in position placed Carroll's understrength command on the right of Brigadier General Alexander Webb's Philadelphia Brigade which was being menaced by the charging Georgians of Brigadier General Ambrose Wright's Brigade as well as some of Brigadier General Carnot Posey's Mississippians. Carroll successfully shifted his command to the assigned position "under a heavy discharge of shot, shell, and musketry."[63]

Carroll's men were in their new position only a short time when General Hays ordered the colonel's command back to its original position. Though the 7th West Virginia and 14th Indiana immediately shifted to the right, the 4th Ohio remained on the left flank of Colonel Smyth's brigade. Lieutenant Colonel Leonard W. Carpenter, commander of the 4th Ohio, recalled that his regiment held this position "for one and a half hours, the whole time exposed to the enemy's artillery and sharpshooters, but being somewhat protected by a fence, the regiment did not suffer greatly."[64] Upon returning to its original position, the 7th West Virginia was "placed

---

[62]Caines, "A Gettysburg Diary"; David H. Beem to Wife, July 5, 1863, United States Army Military History Institute, Carlisle Barracks, Carlisle, Pennsylvania; David Beem, Speech, USAMHI; *O.R.*, vol. 27, part 1, p. 460; "M," "What the 14th Ind. Did."

[63]*O.R.*, vol. 27, part 1, pp. 457, 460; Kepler, ***History of the Three Months***, p. 127; Pfanz, ***The Second Day***, p. 385; Lieutenant Colonel Lockwood of the 7th West Virginia (*O.R.*, vol. 27, part 1, p. 463) wrote that the movement to the left took place at 4:00 p.m.

[64]*Ibid.*, pp. 457, 460, 463.

Lieutenant Colonel Leonard W. Carpenter

Commanded the 4th Ohio Infantry of Colonel Carroll's brigade at Gettysburg.

(*Roger D. Hunt Collection, USAMHI.*)

to protect the Fourth U.S. Artillery, where we remained under heavy fire from the enemy's batteries until about 8 o'clock."[65]

As Colonel Carroll maneuvered his three regiments to the left and then back to the right, the men of the 8th Ohio began to realize just how far removed from the main line back on Cemetery Ridge they were. The Confederate artillery fusillade directed against General Hays' position had been accompanied by a general advance of the grayclad infantry. Many of the Southerners approached the Buckeyes from the woods on Seminary Ridge to the west. Lieutenant Colonel Sawyer also recalled seeing a line of Rebel skirmishers moving on his right flank from the village to the north "keeping well under the cover of fences and buildings." Company D under command of Captain Reid was ordered out of the Emmitsburg Road rifle pit to the aid of the two advanced skirmish companies. Reid's men fixed bayonets and quickly set out toward the advancing Rebel skirmish line. Seeing that one company may not be enough to stop the advancing Southerners, Sawyer ordered the remainder of the regiment to the relief of the skirmishers. This push, combined with galling small arms volleys delivered by Federal skirmishers to the north of the Ohioans' position, as well as artillery fire supplied by batteries on Cemetery Ridge, was enough to repulse the Rebels into and beyond Stevens Run. The 8th Ohio

---

[65]*Ibid.*, p. 463; The only 4th U.S. battery near the northern end of Cemetery Ridge was Lieutenant Alonzo Cushing's Battery A. It is likely that Carroll's men supported this battery when the brigade was shifted to the left. After returning to its original position, the Gibraltar Brigade probably supported Lieutenant Woodruff's Battery I, 1st U.S. Artillery.

J.L. Dickelman of the 4th Ohio (Dickelman, "Gen. Carroll's Gibraltar Brigade") recalled the shift to the left a little differently than most participants; "About 3 p.m. Gen. Carroll was directed to move his command toward the Peach Orchard to support Gen. Sickles, who was being hard pressed by Longstreet at that time. We immediately formed in line and double-quicked to Gen. Sickles's support, remaining in this position till about sundown, when we were ordered to remove to Cemetery Hill." Although Dickelman's statement is basically correct regarding the direction of the movements and the 4th's remaining behind, his and the two other regiments of Carroll's brigade obviously did not move as far left as the Peach Orchard.

suffered 2 men killed and 16 wounded during this short but spirited action.[66]

Not long before dark, the "roar of a line of battle" was heard issuing from the direction of Cemetery Hill.[67] As he rode north toward the right of the Second Corps line, General Hancock sensed that "the firing [seemed] to come nearer and nearer." Joining Brigadier General John Gibbon, temporary commander of the Second Corps, Hancock reportedly remarked to Gibbon; "We ought to send some help over there. Send a brigade, send Carroll!"[68] Gibbon quickly set to issuing orders to dispatch Colonel Carroll's brigade to Eleventh Corps commander General Oliver Otis Howard's assistance. Years after the war, Gibbon recalled that "Carroll...was soon in motion, hurrying his brigade to the sound of the guns."[69]

Colonel Carroll received Gibbon's order through Major J. M. Norvell, the divisional adjutant general. The colonel was directed to "move immediately" to the support of that "part of the Eleventh Corps

---

[66] *O.R.*, vol. 27, part 1, p. 457; Sawyer, *A Military History of the 8th Regiment*, pp. 127-128; "F," "A Spirited Account of the Battle"; Christ, *"Over a Wide, Hot,...Crimson Plain,"* p. 43; Galwey, *Valiant Hours*, p. 103.

[67] John Gibbon, *Personal Recollections of the Civil War* (New York: G.P. Putnam's Sons, reprint edition, Dayton, Ohio: Press of the Morningside Bookshop, 1978), p. 138.

[68] *O.R.*, vol. 27, part 1, p. 372; Command of the Second Corps had been turned over to General Gibbon shortly after the Confederates launched their attack on the Third Corps (*Ibid.*, pp. 416, 417).

[69] *Ibid.*, pp. 372, 417; Gibbon, *Personal Recollections*, p. 138; General Hancock implied in his post-battle report that shortly after Colonel Carroll's men headed off toward East Cemetery Hill, he heard firing on the far right. Believing this to be General Slocum's front, Hancock directed Gibbon to send two regiments to that location. The 71st and 106th Pennsylvania of the Philadelphia Brigade were sent to the right (*O.R.*, vol. 27, part 1, p. 372). Although the 71st Pennsylvania made it to Culp's Hill, the 106th Pennsylvania reported to General Howard, who assigned the regiment to General Ames (*Ibid.*, p. 434; Joseph R.C. Ward, *History of the One Hundred and Sixth Regiment, Pennsylvania Volunteers* (Philadelphia: Grant, Fiares & Rodgers, 1883), p. 163).

supporting batteries on Cemetery Hill, as they were being driven back." The colonel was informed that the Confederates were assaulting the Federal line and that he would be conducted to his assigned position by one of General Howard's aides.[70]

The orders directing Carroll's brigade to the right were relayed to regimental commanders between 7:30 and 8:00 p.m. The bluecoats promptly fell into line, faced right and double-quicked across the Taneytown Road. The men moved off with the colonel at the head of the lead regiment, the 14th Indiana, followed by the 7th West Virginia.[71] The understrength 4th Ohio, having remained on the left flank of Colonel Smyth's brigade, hurried to bring up the rear. The Buckeyes trailed so far behind the 7th that they had to be guided by a Captain Gregg, acting assistant inspector general of Carroll's brigade. Carroll's men presently found themselves "among the tombs and gravestones" of the Evergreen Cemetery. The men moved at the double-quick completely oblivious to what lay ahead. A member of the 4th Ohio recorded that many of the men tossed knapsacks and blankets aside "in order to keep up with the mad rush." Although they had no idea of their destination, Carroll's men knew by the "cannon's vivid flash and thundering roar" up ahead that they were heading into a menacing situation.[72]

While Samuel Carroll led his three regiments toward the Federal right, the 8th Ohio remained in the fields west of the Emmitsburg Road. Their relatively isolated position, however, did not prevent the Buckeyes

---

[70]*Ibid.*, p. 457; Though Colonel Carroll implied that he had a fairly complete understanding of the situation on East Cemetery Hill, the evidence suggests that neither Hancock nor Gibbon comprehended the exact nature of the fighting on the right. Carroll's report was written after he knew why he had been sent to Howard's assistance. The colonel was probably correct in stating that he was to be conducted by one of General Howard's aides although Howard appears not to have directly requested the assistance of Hancock.

[71]*Ibid.*, pp. 457, 459, 463; "M," "What the 14th Ind. Did"; Caines, "A Gettysburg Diary"; Kepler, *History of the Three Months*, pp. 127-128.

[72]Kepler, *History of the Three Months*, pp. 127-128; *O.R.*, vol. 27, part 1, p. 460; Caines, "A Gettysburg Diary"; "M," "What the 14th Ind. Did"; J.L. Dickelman, "Gen. Carroll's Gibraltar Brigade at Gettysburg"; David Beem, Speech, USAMHI.

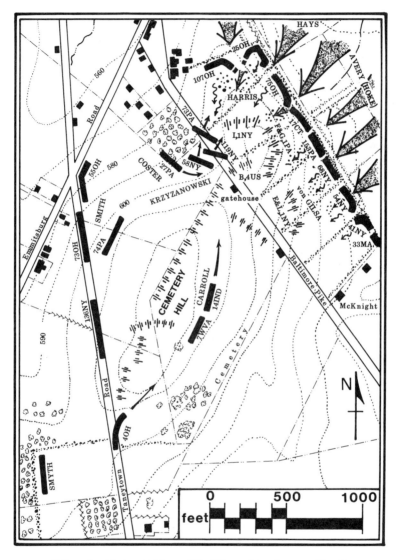

Map 4: Colonel Carroll's Three Regiments Rush to East Cemetery Hill in Response to General Early's Evening Assault

from feeling the effects of the fighting on East Cemetery Hill. Lieutenant Colonel Sawyer recalled that "balls from...rebel batteries on Rock Creek came pouring down among us." Another member of the 8th wrote that "all at once a terrific roar of artillery burst forth from the direction of Culp's Hill....Balls whistled above and around us; splinters of exploded shells struck in our midst; now and then a round shot ricochetted in our vicinity." As if this were not enough, Confederate infantry began forming to the north of the Ohioans' position "as if with the intention of scooping us up." At this point, Sawyer sent word to Colonel Carroll of the 8th's dire predicament. Division commander Hays promptly informed Sawyer that the colonel and the three remaining regiments of the brigade had been sent to the right and that no help could be provided. Hays added that the lieutenant colonel was to hold his position to the last man.[73]

---

[73] Sawyer, *A Military History of the 8th Regiment*, p. 128; "F," "A Spirited Account of the Battle"; Sawyer, *The Eighth Ohio at Gettysburg*, p. 5; Luckily, Sawyer's regiment was not attacked during the night, although they "were constantly harassed by sharp-shooters, whose locality could not be discovered."

CONFEDERATE ASSAULT ON EAST CEMETERY HILL

General Hancock had ordered Colonel Carroll's brigade toward the sound of fighting on the Federal right flank. Although he may not have realized it at the time, the racket that the Second Corps commander had heard was Lieutenant General Richard S. Ewell's assault on Culp's and Cemetery hills.[74] A short time earlier, 19-year-old Major Joseph W. Latimer, division commander Major General Edward "Old Allegheny" Johnson's artillery chief, had been ordered to deploy his battalion along the crest of Benner's Hill to the north and south of the Hanover Road.[75] Sometime between 4:00 and 5:00 p.m. Latimer began shelling Yankee positions on East Cemetery Hill ostensibly in support of General Longstreet's assault of the Federal left flank.[76] Some artillery rounds, especially those fired by the long range 20-pounder Parrotts of one section of Captain C.I. Raine's Lee Battery posted north of the Hanover Road, appear to have travelled completely over Cemetery Hill and landed among the 8th Ohio in the fields west of the Emmitsburg Road. The fusillade continued until about 6:00 p.m. by which time superior numbers of Federal artillery on Culp's and Cemetery hills overwhelmed Latimer's relatively exposed command. The "Boy Major" was ordered to withdraw all of his batteries save one to protect against a possible Federal infantry

---

[74] The reader is referred to Harry Pfanz's excellent account of the fighting on the Federal right (Harry W. Pfanz, *Gettysburg-Culp's Hill and Cemetery Hill* (Chapel Hill, North Carolina: The University of North Carolina Press, 1993)). It is not author's the intent to restate what Pfanz has already covered; rather, the following discussion is intended to simply set the stage for the arrival of Colonel Carroll's men on East Cemetery Hill.

[75] Robert K. Krick, *Lee's Colonels* 4th Edition (Dayton, Ohio: Press of the Morningside Bookshop. 1992), pp. 35, 231; Major Latimer was temporary artillery battalion commander for Lieutenant Colonel Richard Snowden Andrews, who had been wounded in the fighting around Winchester, Virginia.

[76] *O.R.*, vol. 27, part 2, pp. 446, 504; General Ewell recorded that the cannonade began at 5:00 p.m., whereas General Johnson wrote that Latimer's guns opened up one hour earlier.

Lieutenant General Richard S. Ewell

Commanded the Second Corps, Army of Northern Virginia.

(*Library of Congress.*)

attack. Perhaps the Confederates suffered the greatest loss of the artillery exchange when, near its end, Major Latimer was mortally wounded.[77]

"Immediately after the artillery firing ceased," General Ewell instructed division commander Johnson to attack the Federal line on Culp's Hill. As soon as word reached him that Johnson's men were under way, Major General Jubal A. Early ordered Brigadier General Harry T. Hays, who had been placed in overall command of his and Hoke's Brigade, to begin his assault of the east slope of Cemetery Hill. General Hays' five regiments, the 5th, 6th, 7th, 8th and 9th Louisiana, otherwise known as the "Tigers," moved forward somewhat before 8:00 p.m. Colonel Archibald C. Godwin of the 57th North Carolina recorded that Hoke's Brigade, commanded by Colonel Isaac E. Avery and composed of Godwin's regiment and the 6th and 21st North Carolina, was ordered forward at sunset. General Hays' roughly 2,000 men moved forward with the Louisianians on the right and Avery's North Carolinians on the left.[78]

---

[77] *Ibid.*, pp. 446-447, 456, 504, 505; Generals Ewell's and Johnson's estimated times of initiation and duration of the cannonade places its end at approximately 6:00 p.m. This seems too early if the infantry assault started shortly after the end of the cannonade. Details of the July 2 artillery action on the Federal right flank can be found in Pfanz, *Culp's Hill and Cemetery Hill*, pp. 168-189.

[78] *O.R.*, vol. 27, part 2, pp. 447, 480, 483; Coddington, *Gettysburg Campaign*, p. 435; Busey and Martin, *Regimental Strengths*, p. 157; The starting time of General Hays' attack varies from witness to witness. Lieutenant Colonel Detleo von Einsiedel of the 41st New York (*O.R.*, vol. 27, part 1, p. 714) recalled that the assault was made at 6:30 p.m. Major Thomas W. Osborn, artillery chief of the Eleventh Corps (*Ibid.*, p. 747), recorded that the Confederate infantry charged from the town at between 7:00 and 8:00 p.m. Captain John M. Lutz of the 107th Ohio remembered that "At about 7 p.m. the enemy appeared in force" (*Ibid.*, p. 720). First Corps artillery commander Colonel Charles Wainwright wrote that at "about an hour after sundown, the moon shinning brightly, the enemy made a push for our position" (Allan Nevins (editor), *A Diary of Battle: The Personal Journals of Colonel Charles S. Wainwright, 1861-1865* (New York: Harcourt, Brace & World, 1962; reprint edition, Gettysburg: Stan Clark Military Books, 1993), p. 245). The most accurate estimate of the start of the Confederate assault is probably between 7:30 and 8:00 p.m.

The estimated number of men in Hays' attacking columns assumes that roughly 500 men of Hays' and Hoke's brigades were out of action after July 1.

Major General Jubal A. Early

Commanded a division in the Second Corps, Army of Northern Virginia at Gettysburg. Early's brigades assaulted Federal positions on East Cemetery Hill on the evening of July 2.

(*Library of Congress.*)

Brigadier General Harry T. Hays

General Hays' Louisiana "Tigers" occupied the right wing of the Confederate force that assaulted East Cemetery Hill. He was given field command of the attack.

*(Francis Trevelyan Miller, editor, **The Photographic History of the Civil War in Ten Volumes**. New York: The Review of Reviews, Co., 1911, vol. 10.)*

Colonel Isaac E. Avery

Commanded Hoke's Brigade of three North Carolina regiments during the assault of East Cemetery Hill. Avery's regiments held the left wing of General Hays' Confederate force. The colonel was mortally wounded during the assault.

(*North Carolina Division of Archives and History, Department of Cultural Resources.*)

The Southern infantry approached Eleventh Corps troops deployed along a stone fence bordering a lane at the base of East Cemetery Hill. These men comprised General Howard's First Division commanded by Brigadier General Adelbert Ames, who had replaced the wounded Brigadier General Francis C. Barlow. Ames' left flank was anchored by his own brigade, now commanded by Colonel Andrew L. Harris of the 75th Ohio. The brigade included, from left to right, the 107th Ohio, 25th Ohio, 17th Connecticut, and 75th Ohio. The entire 107th and probably the right wing of the 25th appears to have faced north along a stone fence that intersected the lane at a right angle.[79] On Harris' left were the four regiments of Colonel Leopold von Gilsa's brigade, the 54th and 68th New York, 153rd Pennsylvania, and 41st New York. Von Gilsa's brigade had been badly served at Chancellorsville where they had received the initial shock of Stonewall Jackson's lightning attack on May 2. The four regiments included many German immigrants and soldiers of German lineage, a fact that was not lost on many of the officers of the Army of the Potomac.[80] General Ames' brigades, which had still not

---

[79]*O.R.*, vol. 27, part 1, p. 714; Pfanz, *Culp's Hill and Cemetery Hill*, p. 238; Andrew L. Harris to John Bachelder, April 7, 1864, *in* Ladd and Ladd, *Bachelder Papers*, 1: 138; Captain John Lutz of the 107th Ohio recalled that his regiment had been posted behind a board fence (*O.R.*, vol. 27, part 1, p. 720). Captain Peter F. Young, adjutant of this regiment, mistakenly believed that the 25th Ohio was on the left of the 107th (Peter F. Young to John Bachelder, August 12, 1867, *in* Ladd and Ladd, *Bachelder Papers*, 1: 311). Only a part of the stone fence held by the 107th and 25th Ohio can be seen on the battlefield today.

[80]Von Gilsa's regiments went by such names as the "DeKalb Regiment" (41st New York) and "Schwarzer Jaeger" or "Black Rifles" (54th New York). The New York regiments were all originally commanded by native Germans who had served in various military capacities in Europe. The 153rd Pennsylvania was organized in Northampton County, Pennsylvania, an area of the Keystone State inhabited by a sizeable "Pennsylvania Dutch" population (Edmund J. Raus, Jr., *A Generation on the March-The Union Army at Gettysburg* (Lynchburg, Virginia: H.E. Howard, Inc., 1987), pp. 59, 62, 68, 140; New York Monuments Commission for the Battlefields of Gettysburg and Chattanooga, *Final Report on the Battlefield of Gettysburg*, 3 volumes, Edited by William F. Fox (Albany, New York: J.B. Lyon Company, Printers, 1902), 1: 397 (herein referred to as *New York at Gettysburg*).

Brigadier General Adelbert Ames

When the fighting started at Gettysburg of July 1, General Ames was in command of the Second Brigade of Brigadier General Francis C. Barlow's first Division of the Eleventh Corps. When Barlow was wounded that day, Ames assumed division command.

(*USAMHI.*)

Colonel Andrew L. Harris

Original commander of the 75th Ohio Infantry, Colonel Harris ascended to command of the Second Brigade, First Division of the Eleventh Corps, when General Ames took division command.

(*MOLLUS Collection, USAMHI.*)

View of Gettysburg

July 1863 image (view to the north toward Gettysburg) showing ground over which the "Louisiana Tigers" attacked the 107th Ohio and right wing of the 25th Ohio, both of which occupied the low stone fence along which the tall trees can be seen. Eventually the Ohioans were forced to withdraw to the closer stone fence.

(*Library of Congress.*)

Colonel Leopold von Gilsa

Commanded the First Brigade of the First Division, Eleventh Corps, Army of the Potomac. His four New York and Pennsylvania regiments, along with the 33rd Massachusetts, held the right of the Federal line on East Cemetery Hill on July 2.

(*MOLLUS Collection, USAMHI.*)

recovered from the fighting on the plains north of Gettysburg the day before, would be sorely tested this evening.

The 33rd Massachusetts, detached from Colonel Orland Smith's Second Brigade of Brigadier General Adolph von Steinwehr's Second Division formed on the right flank of the 41st New York. Earlier in the day, these regiments had joined Companies A and F of the 153rd Pennsylvania deployed in a skirmish line 500 to 600 yards to the front of the base of East Cemetery Hill. The skirmishers volleyed at General Hays' approaching troops and began falling back to the stone fence at the base of the hill, stopping several times to fire at the approaching Southerners.[81]

---

[81]*O.R.*, vol. 27, part 1, pp. 714, 722; Pfanz, *Culp's Hill and Cemetery Hill*, p. 238; *New York at Gettysburg*, 1: p. 404; David G. Martin, *Carl Bornemann's Regiment: The Forty-First New York Infantry* (Hightstown, New Jersey: Longstreet House, 1987), p. 150; W.R. Keifer, *History of the One Hundred and Fifty-third Regiment Pennsylvania Volunteers* (Easton, Pennsylvania: Press of the Chemical Publishing Co., 1909), p. 141; J. Clyde Miller to John B. Bachedler, March 2, 1884, *in* Ladd and Ladd, *Bachelder Letters*, 2: 1026. Harry Pfanz discussed the initial deployment and redeployment of Harris' and von Gilsa's regiments (Pfanz, *Culp's Hill and Cemetery Hill*, pp. 247-249). The positioning of the latter's regiments is difficult to assess because they did not form a line until the attack was under way. A map in Pfanz's book (*Ibid*, p. 238) shows the order of regiments from left to right to be the 153rd Pennsylvania, 68th and 54th New York and 41st New York. Martin, apparently referring to the placement of the regimental monuments, John Bachelder's July 2, 1863 Troop Position Map and Lieutenant Colonel von Einsiedel's post-battle report, interpreted the arrangement of von Gilsa's regiments to be, from left to right, the 54th and 68th New York, 153rd Pennsylvania and the 41st New York (Martin, *Carl Bornemann's Regiment*, p. 151; *O.R.*, vol 27, part 1, p. 714; Troop Position Map, July 2, 1863, *in* Ladd and Ladd, *Bachelder Papers*). Lieutenant J. Clyde Miller of Company A, 153rd Pennsylvania, recalled that when he and others of the regiment fell back to the Federal line at the bottom of the hill, they were informed by members of the 41st New York (who must have reached the stone fence before the Pennsylvanians returned) that the 153rd had moved toward the left flank of the line (Keifer, *One Hundred and Fifty-third*, p. 141; J. Clyde Miller to John B. Bachedler, March 2, 1884, *in* Ladd and Ladd, *Bachelder Letters*, 2: p. 1026). This would seem to support Pfanz's interpretation of the arrangement of von Gilsa's regiments.

Brigadier General Adolph von Steinwehr

Commanded the Second Division of the Eleventh Corps, Army of the Potomac. Several regiments of his command would be instrumental in repulsing Confederate infantry from Captain Wiedrich's battery.

(MOLLUS Collection, USAMHI.)

A bit to the right of the 33rd Massachusetts were Captain Greenlief T. Stevens' six Napoleons of the 5th Maine Battery situated on a prominence between Culp's and Cemetery Hills. Lieutenant Edward N. Whittier was in command of the battery after Captain Stevens had been wounded that morning. The Eleventh Corps infantry regiments deployed along the stone fence at the base of East Cemetery Hill were supported by Captain Michael Wiedrich's four 3-inch Ordnance rifles of Battery I, 1st New York Light Artillery and the six 3-inch Ordnance Rifles of combined Batteries F and G, 1st Pennsylvania Light Artillery, commanded by Captain R. Bruce Ricketts. The Pennsylvania battery was positioned on Wiedrich's immediate right and in front of the Evergreen Cemetery gate. A bit farther to the right and down the hill were the five 3-inch Ordnance Rifles of combined Batteries E and L, 1st New York Light Artillery, under the command of Lieutenant George Breck. The four remaining Napoleons of Lieutenant James B. Stewart's Battery B, 4th United States Artillery, were deployed across the Baltimore Pike in front of the cemetery gate facing north toward Gettysburg.[82]

General Hays' line of Louisianians and North Carolinians would have to angle to the right to strike the Federal troops along the base of East Cemetery Hill. Such a maneuver was difficult enough on a parade ground let alone under fire. The grayclad soldiers emerged from the cover of woods onto a relatively open, rolling field cut by several ravines. It was at this point that the Northern skirmish line fired and fell back to the base of the hill. General Hays wheeled his "Tigers" toward the left flank

---

[82]Coddington, *Gettysburg Campaign*, p. 435; *O.R.*, vol. 27, part 1, pp. 361, 722; Martin, *Bornemann's Regiment*, p. 151; On July 1, General Howard had requested that Colonel Wainwright, First Corps artillery commander, take orders directly from Howard; Eleventh Corps artillery chief, Major Thomas W. Osborn, would then take orders from Wainwright. Both artillery officers discussed the situation and agreed that Osborn would command the batteries west of the Baltimore Pike and Wainwright would take charge of those east of the pike, including the batteries on East Cemetery Hill (Nevins, *A Diary of Battle*, p. 237; *O.R.*, vol. 27, part 1, p. 748; Thomas W. Osborn, "The Artillery at Gettysburg," *Philadelphia Weekly Times*, May 31, 1879).

**Terrain Over Which the North Carolinians
Marched Toward East Cemetery Hill**

Hummocky terrain over which Colonel Isaac Avery's North Carolinians marched toward the Federal line at the base of East Cemetery Hill (left horizon). Early on July 2, 1863, Federal troops of the 41st New York, 33rd Massachusetts and 153rd Pennsylvania were deployed as skirmishers in these fields. The Northerners were driven back to the base of the hill as General Hays' troops began their assault.

of Ames' line. As the Rebels crested a low ridge they immediately encountered shot and shell delivered by Yankee artillerymen on the hill.[83]

Colonel Avery's three North Carolina regiments, marching almost parallel to the Federal line had to execute a right wheel in order to strike the Yankees head on. As soon as the Rebels come into view, Colonel Charles Wainwright ordered Lieutenant Whittier of the 5th Maine Battery to open up on the Confederate line. The Maine artillerymen delivered a withering fire of canister into Colonel Avery's North Carolina regiments. The Tarheels were also hit by small arms fire delivered by the 33rd Massachusetts and the right wing of the 41st New York. Colonel Avery was mortally wounded in this salvo, yet his resolute men "came on and on."[84]

The rifles of Weidrich's, Ricketts' and Breck's batteries combined with those of the Maine battery to exact a terrible toll on the oncoming Rebels. An artilleryman with Ricketts' battery claimed that Southern troops "fell dead before the iron storm at the rate of a dozen a minute." Ricketts' men fired canister at a rate of one round every 15 seconds. Nevertheless, the Rebels came on "with the precision of a parade and all the steadiness of a holiday spectacle." Colonel Harris recalled that Early's men "moved forward as steadily, amid this hail of shot and shell and minnie ball as though they were on parade far removed from danger." The colonel also expressed astonishment that the Confederate attack actually occurred. Years after the battle, he wrote that the assault against East Cemetery Hill "was a complete surprise to us. We did not expect this assault as bravely and rapidly made. In fact, we did not expect any assault[.]"[85]

---

[83]Pfanz, *Culp's Hill and Cemetery Hill*, p. 238; Coddington, *Gettysburg Campaign*, p. 435; *O.R.*, vol. 27, part 1, p. 358.

[84]Coddington, *Gettysburg Campaign*, p. 435; Walter Clark (compiler), *Histories of the Several Regiments and Battalions from North Carolina in the Great War 1861-65*, 5 volumes (Raleigh and Goldsboro, North Carolina: State of North Carolina, 1901), 1: 316.

[85]L.E.C. Moore, "Charge of the Louisianians," *National Tribune*, August 5, 1909; Nevins, *Diary of Battle*, p. 245; Andrew L. Harris to John Bachelder, March 14, *in* Ladd and Ladd, *Bachelder Papers*, 2: 745.

Colonel Charles S. Wainwright

Original commander of Battery I, 1st New York Light Artillery, Colonel Wainwright commanded the First Corps Artillery Brigade at Gettysburg.

(*USAMHI.*)

Stevens' 5th Maine Battery

Pencil and wash drawing by Alfred R. Waud of Captain Greenlief T. Stevens' 5th Maine Battery firing on Colonel Avery's troops. The Evergreen Cemetery Gatehouse can be seen in the background.

(*Library of Congress.*)

General Ames' line was seriously weakened only a few moments into the Confederate assault when he ordered Harris to shift the 17th Connecticut, under command of Major Allen G. Brady, to the right of the brigade, apparently to close a gap between Harris' and von Gilsa's commands. The removal of the 17th left only a small number of the 25th Ohio to cover that part of the line vacated by the Nutmeg regiment thereby endangering the right flank of that regiment and the left of the 75th Ohio. Harris attempted to correct the flaw in his line by holding the left flank of the 107th stationary and stretching that regiment and the 25th to the left. Fully realizing his perilous situation, Harris rode along his "very thin and weak line" giving "the men all the encouragement possible."[86]

Shortly after Major Brady reported to von Gilsa, the Confederate column came into view. When the Southerners had drawn to within about 150 paces of the stone fence at the base of the hill, Federal infantrymen rose and began firing. Brady wrote that "we poured a destructive fire upon them, which thinned their ranks and checked their advance." He declared that his men "fired several volleys by battalion" after which the Rebels charged the stone fence. The volume of small arms fire delivered by the bluecoats appears to have varied along the line. Whereas L. Eugene C. Moore of Ricketts' Battery G recalled seeing Northern infantrymen unleash "volley after volley into the faces of the Tigers," other men such as Captain Ricketts and his subordinate Lieutenant Charles Brockway claimed that the Eleventh Corps riflemen fired very little.[87]

---

[86] *O.R.*, vol. 27, part 1, pp. 715, 718, 720; Martin, ***Bornemann's Regiment***, p. 150; Andrew L. Harris to John Bachelder, April 7, 1864, *in* Ladd and Ladd, ***Bachelder Papers***, p. 138; Andrew L. Harris to John Bachelder, March 14, 1881, *in Ibid*, 2: 745, 746.

[87] Moore, "Charge of the Louisianians"; *O.R.*, vol. 27, part 1, p. 718; R. Bruce Ricketts to John Bachelder, March 2, 1866, *in* Ladd and Ladd, ***Bachelder Papers***, 1: 236; Charles B. Brockway to David McConaughy, March 5, 1864, Peter F. Rothermal Papers, Pennsylvania State Archives, Harrisburg, Pennsylvania; A member of the 153rd Pennsylvania recalled that Colonel von Gilsa, standing a short distance in the rear of his line at the stone fence, believed that the advancing Confederates were actually Northern skirmishers and ordered his men to cease firing (Keifer, ***One Hundred and Fifty-third***, p. 141).

Major Allen G. Brady

On July 2, Major Brady commanded the 17th Connecticut Infantry.

(Bridgeport Public Library, Bridgeport, Connecticut.)

Colonel Harris' thinned line was in great danger. The right flank of Hays' brigade, advancing from the north, collided with the 107th Ohio. The Buckeyes were soon overpowered and ordered to fall back upon Weidrich's battery. Captain John Lutz recalled that his men fought the Louisianians as they retired toward a stone fence near the battery. While retreating, the 107th's color-sergeant was shot. Captain Peter Young retrieved the flag and carried it back to a second stone fence near the New York battery. As the exultant Southerners drove the Ohioans from the first stone fence toward Captain Weidrich's battery, they passed "such of the enemy who had not fled, and who were still clinging for shelter to the wall."[88]

Though their supports on the left were giving way, the men of the 17th Connecticut displayed a dogged determination to hold the line along the stone fence at the base of the hill. The fighting was hand-to-hand but the blueclad troops stayed with it. During this confused action Major Brady was wounded. While the Nutmeg regiment battled with the "Tigers," Colonel von Gilsa's regiments were being pressed by the left flank of Hays' Brigade as well as Tarheels of Hoke's Brigade. The Rebels drove the 54th and part of the 68th New York away from the stone fence. The men of the 153rd Pennsylvania, however, tenaciously held their places on the wavering line. Lieutenant Miller recalled that the Pennsylvania regiment fought "in all its fierceness, muskets being handled as clubs; rocks torn from the wall in front and thrown, fists and bayonets used, so close was the fighting." A Southern flag-bearer climbed on the stone fence, spread his arms and shouted "Surrender, you damned Yankees." One of the Pennsylvanians ran his bayonet through the man's

---

[88]*O.R.*, vol. 27, part 1, p. 720; *Ibid.*, part 2, p. 480; Peter F. Young to John Bachelder, August 12, 1867, *in* Ladd and Ladd, ***Bachelder Papers***, 1: 311; Alfred J. Rider to John Bachelder, August 20, 1885, *In Ibid.*, 2: 119; The stone fence toward which the 107th Ohio retreated is probably that low fence which can now been seen on the immediate left of Weidrich's position.

Alfred Rider of the 107th recalled that the flag-bearer had been shot in the wrist and that the ball lodged near the man's elbow. Rider recorded that his wounded comrade "walked around the 11th Corps Hospital several days, and wouldn't let the Dr's cut out the ball. I plead with him one evening when he was frying potatoes and onions to have the ball extracted. He swore he wouldn't and the next morning he was dead. We buried him." (Alfred J. Rider to John Bachelder, October 3, 1885, *in Ibid.*, 2: 1129)

chest as he pulled the trigger of his Austrian rifle musket. More than 40 years after the battle, Miller recalled "how the shot tore into shreds the back of his blouse." There was a scramble for the fallen colors, which the Rebels apparently won. Finally the strength of Southern numbers compelled the 153rd and the 68th New York on the right to retreat up the slope toward Captain Ricketts' battery.[89]

The final collapse of von Gilsa's line compelled the 5th Maine battery to cease firing at this time for fear of hitting Yankee infantrymen mingling with Confederates on the slope of the hill. Nevertheless, the Southerners who had penetrated the disrupted Union line found the going anything but easy. Indeed, Colonel A.C. Godwin, who had assumed command of Hoke's Brigade after Avery was wounded, wrote that his men "became much separated, and in the darkness it was now found impossible to concentrate more than 40 or 50 men at any point for a farther advance."[90]

Federal soldiers were now withdrawing up the east slope of Cemetery Hill toward the batteries. In order to stem this tide, some of Lieutenant Stewart's batterymen were deployed along the Baltimore Pike and armed with fence rails to keep men and officers from running away. Colonel Wainwright complained that General Ames' men "would not stand at all" and "ran away almost to a man."[91] Although this severe indictment of the entire First Division of the Eleventh Corps was patently incorrect, it would serve as the basis for the post-war debate that would continue for more than 50 years.

The right wing of the Louisiana brigade worked its way up the north face of the hill toward Captain Weidrich's battery. They soon found themselves battling German artillerymen armed with sponge-staffs, stones,

---

[89]*New York at Gettysburg*, vol. 1, pp. 308, 404; *Ibid.*, vol. 2, p. 568; *O.R.*, vol. 27, part 1, pp. 714, 718; M. Browne to John Bachelder, April 8, 1864, *in* Ladd and Ladd, ***Bachelder Papers***, 1: 149; Keifer, ***One Hundred and Fifty-third***, pp. 141-142.

[90]*O.R.*, vol. 27, part 2, p. 484; Moore, "Charge of the Louisianians"

[91]Nevins, *A Diary of Battle*, p. 245.

View of Stevens' Knoll and Culp's Hill

View to the southeast from the 4th Ohio monument on East Cemetery Hill, toward Stevens' Knoll (center horizon) and Culp's Hill (left). The position of combined Batteries E and L, 1st New York Light Artillery, is visible on the right. North Carolinians of Colonel Isaac Avery's (Hoke's) brigade assaulted Colonel Leopold von Gilsa's men deployed in a line that approximately ran along modern Wainwright Avenue. The McKnight house is visible above the lunettes.

handspikes and fence-rails.[92] The men of the 107th Ohio had fallen back to Weidrich's battery where they found "the rebels up to and among our guns, yelling like demons at the supposed capture." Buckeye Captain Peter Young, who took it upon himself the rally some of the disorganized Yankee infantry and artillerymen, charged toward the battery with revolver drawn and shot the color-bearer of the 8th Louisiana. Young snatched the "vile rag" from the fallen Rebel and started back toward his regiment when the captain was shot in the left lung. Surprisingly the wounded Yankee was able to stagger back to his line with his trophy. Possibly inspired by this act of bravery, the 107th battled courageously from behind a stone fence, probably on the left flank of Weidrich's pieces.[93]

Fortunately for the besieged New York battery, infantry help was not far away. The start of the Confederate infantry advance against East Cemetery Hill found General Howard standing with his Third Division commander Major General Carl Schurz on the north face of the hill in the rear of Schurz's line. Shortly before 8:00 p.m. the two officers heard the clamor on the east slope build.[94] General Schurz, at the behest of his corps commander, ordered the two closest regiments, the 58th and 119th New York, to fix bayonets. The New York regiments, under overall command of Colonel Wladimir Krzyzanowski and accompanied by

---

[92]Coddington, *Gettysburg Campaign*, p. 436; Cyrus Kingsbury Remington, *A Record of Battery I, First N.Y. Light Artillery Vols. otherwise known as Wiedrich's Battery during the War of the Rebellion, 1861-'65* (Buffalo, New York: Press of the Courier Company, 1891), p. 28; Nevins, *A Diary of Battle*, pp. 245-246; *O.R.*, vol. 27, part 1, p. 752; *New York at Gettysburg*, 3: p. 1247.

[93]*O.R.*, vol. 27, part 1, p. 720; Captain Young was carried to a water pump near the entrance to the Evergreen Cemetery where water "somewhat allayed the burning fever and saved" his life. The captain was never able to determine the fate of the Rebel colors once they were delivered to Eleventh Corps headquarters (Peter F. Young to John Bachelder, August 12, 1867, *in* Ladd and Ladd, *Bachelder Papers*, 1: 311-312).

[94]Carl Schurz, *The Reminiscences of Carl Schurz*, 3 volumes (New York: McClure Company, 1907-8), 3: 25; Remington, *Weidrich's Battery*, p. 28; Captain Emil Koenig wrote (*O.R.*, vol. 27, part 1, p. 740) that his regiment, the 58th New York, was ordered to the aid of Weidrich's battery at about 8:00 p.m.

Major General Carl Schurz

Commander of the Third Division of the Eleventh Corps, on July 1, General Schurz was assigned command of the corps for General Howard who had taken command of all troops on the field for the morally wounded General John F. Reynolds.

(*MOLLUS Collection, USAMHI.*)

Schurz and his staff, double-quicked across the Baltimore Pike in the gathering darkness toward Weidrich's imperiled battery.[95] As the party rode toward the battery, Schurz recalled that

> soon we found ourselves surrounded by a rushing crowd of stragglers from the already broken lines. We did our best, sword in hand, to drive them back as we went.

Near the battery the general and his aides

> found an indescribable scene of melee. Some rebel infantry had scaled the breastworks, and were taking possession of the guns. But the cannoneers defended themselves desperately.[96]

The 58th and 119th New York were assisted in their mission by Colonel Charles R. Coster's First Brigade of von Steinwehr's division. These regiments, the 27th and 73rd Pennsylvania, and 134th New York, along with Krzyzanowski's two regiments, became embroiled in "a short and very spirited hand-to-hand fight" that helped push the "Tigers" out of Weidrich's battery and down the hill.[97]

---

[95]*Ibid.*, p. 731; *New York at Gettysburg*, vol. 1: 431.

[96]Schurz, *Reminiscences*, 3: p. 25.

[97]Remington, *Weidrich's Battery*, p. 28; Coddington, *Gettysburg Campaign*, p. 436; *New York at Gettysburg*, 2: p. 913; Pennsylvania Gettysburg Battlefield Commission. *Pennsylvania at Gettysburg. Ceremonies at the Dedication of the Monuments Erected by the Commonwealth of Pennsylvania to Mark the Positions of the Pennsylvania Commands Engaged in the Battle.* 2 volumes. John P. Nicholson, editor (Harrisburg, Pennsylvania: W.S. Ryan, State Printers, 1904), 1: 199, 418 (herein referred to as *Pennsylvania at Gettysburg*). *O.R.*, vol. 27, part 1, p. 722; General Schurz (*Ibid.*, p. 731) proudly and correctly proclaimed that his infantry had played a pivotal role in driving the Rebels from Weidrich's guns. Captain Weidrich himself stated that the 73rd Pennsylvania was on the left of the battery and aided in the repulse of the Confederates (quoted in Remington, *Weidrich's Battery*, p. 30). Captain Koenig of the 58th New York, on the other hand, wrote that the Rebels were "repulsed before we arrived" (*O.R.*, vol. 27, part 1, p. 740). Evidently, the 136th New York of Colonel Orland Smith's brigade, von Steinwehr's division,

The fray among the rifles of Captain Weidrich's battery uncovered the left flank of Captain Ricketts' Battery. Almost three years after the battle, Ricketts reminisced that shortly after going into position on Cemetery Hill on the evening of July 2, Colonel Wainwright announced to him:

> Captain, this is the key to our position on Cemetery Hill, and must be held and in case you are charged here, you will not limber up under any circumstances, but fight your battery as long as you can.[98]

Ricketts, a native Pennsylvanian, was about to face this prospect.

A number of "Tigers" had successfully driven through Weidrich's battery and were nearing the low stone fence on the left of Captain Ricketts' position.[99] These men unleashed several ragged volleys as they

---

was also sent to East Cemetery Hill but arrived after the Rebels had been repulsed (*Ibid.*, p. 726). Interestingly, Captain M. Browne, adjutant to General Ames, believed that the Rebels were repulsed from Weidrich's battery only by troops of the First (Ames') Division. Browne wrote that the men sent "from other divisions were of no service" (M. Browne to John Bachelder, April 8, 1864, *in* Ladd and Ladd, ***Bachelder Papers***, 1: 149).

[98]R. Bruce Ricketts to John Bachelder, March 2, 1866, *in* Ladd and Ladd, ***Bachelder Papers***, 1: 237; Captain Ricketts recalled the statement a little differently at the dedication of his commands' battlefield monument: "If a charge is made on this point you will not limber up and leave under any circumstances, but fight your battery as long as you can" (***Pennsylvania at Gettysburg***, 2: 921).

At about 4:30 p.m., shortly after the early evening cannonade, Ricketts' battery relieved Captain James H. Cooper's Battery B, 1st Pennsylvania Light Artillery, which had sustained damage on this day as well as in action on July 1. Colonel Wainwright ordered Cooper's battery to report to the Artillery Reserve to refit and resupply their ammunition chests (***O.R***, vol. 27, part 1, p. 365; R. Bruce Ricketts to W.S. Hancock, December 28, 1885, *in* Ladd and Ladd, ***Bachelder Papers***, 2: 1172; R. Bruce Ricketts to John Bachelder, December 3, 1883, *in Ibid.*, p. 980).

[99]***Pennsylvania at Gettysburg***, 1: 420; Coddington, ***Gettysburg Campaign***, p. 436; Clark, ***Histories of the Several Regiments and Battalions***, 1: 316; ***O.R.***, vol. 27, p. 358.

Captain R. Bruce Ricketts

Command combined Batteries F and G, 1st Pennsylvania Light Artillery. It was this battery that was in danger of being overrun when Colonel Carroll's men arrived in, what one member of the battery recalled was "the nick of time."

(*USAMHI.*)

headed toward the artillery pieces. Oney F. Sweet, a member of the crew working the left piece, saw the approaching Confederates by the flashes of their guns.[100] Some of the Rebels captured and spiked Ricketts' left piece. They continued along the battery, fighting hand-to-hand with the artillerymen, as far as the third gun.[101] The Louisianians were joined by perhaps as many as 75 North Carolinians who were able to assault the artillery pieces from the front. One of the Tarheels may have planted his regimental colors among Captain Ricketts' guns.[102]

Like Weidrich's batterymen, Captain Ricketts' men found themselves in a fierce hand-to-hand fight in the gloom.[103] Some of the outnumbered artillerymen began to falter, but quickly rallied themselves shouting "Death on our own State soil rather than give the enemy the guns!" The frenzied battery crews battled the Southerners with stones, handspikes, rammers and pistols.[104] Captain Moore provided a vivid account of the tumult in and around the battery:

---

[100]Oney F. Sweet, "Ricketts's Battery," *National Tribune*, April 29, 1909.

[101]*O.R.*, vol. 27, part 1, p. 894; Moore, "Charge of the Louisianians"; *Pennsylvania at Gettysburg*, 2: 921; Brigadier General Robert O. Tyler, commanding the artillery reserve, reported that two of Ricketts' guns had been held by the Rebels although only one was spiked (*O.R.*, vol. 27, part 1, p. 873). A member of the 14th Indiana maintained that two of Ricketts' guns were spiked ("M," "What the 14th Ind. Did"); Ricketts himself entered in his pocket diary that his left gun had been spiked and that six batterymen had been killed, three wounded and three taken prisoner (R. Bruce Ricketts to John Bachelder, December 3, 1883, *in* Ladd and Ladd, *Bachelder Letters*, 2: 980).

[102]*O.R.*, vol. 27, part 2, p. 486; Colonel A.C. Godwin reported that part of the 6th North Carolina and the 9th Louisiana "succeeded in capturing a battery on the right." He appears to have been referring to Ricketts' battery (*Ibid.*, p. 485).

[103]Lieutenant Charles B. Brockway of Ricketts' battery recalled that it was "quite dark" by the time the Confederates reached the battery (Charles B. Brockway to David McConaughy, March 5, 1864, Rothermel Papers, Pennsylvania State Archives).

[104]Coddington, *Gettysburg Campaign*, p. 436; Pennsylvania at Gettysburg, 2: p. 921; *O.R.*, vol. 27, part 1, p. 894; Charles B. Brockway to David McConaughy, March 5, 1864, Pennsylvania State Archives; Moore, "Charge of

A struggle takes place for the [battery] guidon; it is in the hands of a 'Tiger.' Lieut. Brockway seizes a stone, hurls it full at the head of the soldier, which fells him to the ground, and in a moment the 'Tiger' is shot with his own musket by Serg't Dick Stratford. The wildest confusion (a bedlam of terror) now ensues."[105]

Lieutenant Brockway declared that "The scene was now one of wildest confusion." It was almost impossible to tell friend from foe. Although the stubborn batterymen had succeeded in checking the Rebels for a moment, they soon found themselves "being overpowered by their desperate and maddened assailants." As Captain Moore put it, "The moment is most critical; the fate of the issue is near at hand."[106]

---

the Louisianians"; J.E. Murdock of the 7th West Virginia recalled that he saw one of Ricketts' batterymen kill a Confederate with a rock taken from the Baltimore Pike (J.E. Murdock, "On Cemetery Hill," *National Tribune*, July 29, 1909); Captain Ricketts believed that some of his men began to fall back from their rifles when they heard orders to retreat shouted to Eleventh Corps infantrymen in front of the battery. After this, Ricketts declared, the batterymen "gave no sign of retreat, but every man did his duty" (R. Bruce Ricketts to John Bachelder, March 2, 1866, *in* Ladd and Ladd, *Bachelder Papers*, 1: 237).

[105] Moore, "Charge of the Louisianians."

[106] Charles B. Brockway to David McConaughy, March 5, 1864, Pennsylvania State Archives; Moore, "Charge of the Louisianians"; *O.R.*, vol. 27, part 1, p. 894.

Second Lieutenant Charles F. Brockway, Ricketts' Battery

(*Dave Richards Collection, USAMHI.*)

CARROLL'S BRIGADE ARRIVES
AT RICKETTS' BATTERY

While a good part of what has been described above was transpiring, Colonel Carroll was leading his three regiments through the Evergreen Cemetery. As the westerners double-quicked toward the Federal right, they encountered a number of men fleeing the east slope of Cemetery Hill. Captain David Beem of the 14th Indiana threatened these men with death on the spot if they did not return to the battle line; his threats had no effect.[107]

General Hancock had dispatched Carroll's command to the right with "no precise orders" regarding where the colonel was to go. On his way across the cemetery, Carroll encountered Captain James F. Huntington, an acquaintance and commander of an Artillery Reserve brigade positioned on Cemetery Hill, which included Captain Ricketts' battery. Huntington provided Carroll with some idea of where the colonel was needed, after which Carroll, in a voice loud enough to be heard over the bedlam, ordered his men toward the threatened batteries.[108] No doubt the bluecoats were also guided to the imperiled part of the Federal line by the flash of small arms fire in the darkness. The arrival of the Gibraltar Brigade at the Baltimore Pike was described by a member of the 33rd Massachusetts who recalled seeing "a dark mass [Carroll's regiments]...move up at the doublequick, onto the flank of the rebels this side."[109]

---

[107]Murdock, "On Cemetery Hill"; David Beem, "History of the Fourteenth Indiana Volunteers," Beem Papers, Indiana Historical Society Library, Indianapolis, Indiana.

[108]Captain J.F. Huntington to General Gibbon, March 26, 1864, cited in Coddington, *Gettysburg Campaign*, p. 437 (fn. 131, p. 766); Baxter, *Gallant Fourteenth*, p. 150.

[109]"M", "What the 14th Ind. Did"; *O.R.*, vol. 27, part 1, p. 457; Adin B. Underwood, *The Three Years Service of the Thirty-Third Massachusetts Infantry, 1862-1865* (Boston: A. Williams & Company, Publishers, 1881), p. 130.

Colonel Carroll's men arrived at the eastern edge of the Evergreen Cemetery to a scene "of wildest confusion."[110] The colonel "found the enemy up to and some of them in among the front guns of the batteries."[111] Through the darkness and smoke, David Beem was able to discern Ricketts' artillerymen fighting the Rebels with their battery tools. Carroll, in a clarion voice, ordered his regiments into battle line. The 14th Indiana crossed the Baltimore Pike just south of the Evergreen Cemetery gate.[112]

Colonel Coons promptly formed the Hoosiers from column into line and bellowed out the command; "By the left flank, march; charge bayonets!" The line lurched toward the Southerners fighting among Ricketts' guns. One Indianian claimed that some of Ricketts' men shouted and tossed their hats in the air as the Hoosiers neared the battery. An officer of the battery "called out 'what regiment is that?', when informed it was the 14th Indiana he [proclaimed] 'God Bless the 14th Indiana.'"[113] Coons' men "met the enemy among the batteries" and found themselves immersed in what one man recalled was a "close and deadly conflict."

---

[110]Charles B. Brockway to David McConaughy, March 5, 1864, Pennsylvania State Archives; W.H. Thurston, "A Ricketts Batterymen Supports Carroll's Brigade Claim, *National Tribune*, October 3, 1892; Moore, "Charge of the Louisianians"; David Beem to Wife, July 5, 1863, USAMHI; Sweet, "Ricketts's Battery"; *Pennsylvania at Gettysburg*, 2: 922.

[111]*O.R.*, vol. 27, part 1, p. 457; It appears that Colonel Carroll's brigade arrived on East Cemetery Hill just as the Eleventh Corps reinforcements swept the Louisianians from Weidrich's battery (Underwood, *Three Years Service*, p. 131).

[112]David Beem, Speech, USAMHI; David Beem to Wife, July 5, 1863, USAMHI; Samuel W. Fiske (editor), *Mr. Dunn Browne's Experiences in the Army* (New York: Nichols and Noyes, 1866), p. 195; Caines, "A Gettysburg Diary"; "M", "What the 14th Ind. Did"; Moore, "Charge of the Louisianians"; *O.R.*, vol. 27, part 1, pp. 459, 460; Dickelman, "Gen. Carroll's Gibraltar Brigade."

[113]*O.R.*, vol. 27, part 1, p. 459; David Beem, Speech, USAMHI; David Beem to Wife, July 5, 1863, USAMHI; "M," "What the 14th Ind. Did"; Another member of the 14th Indiana recalled that a batteryman shouted, "Glory to God. We are saved," as the Hoosiers neared the rifles (Caines, "A Gettysburg Diary").

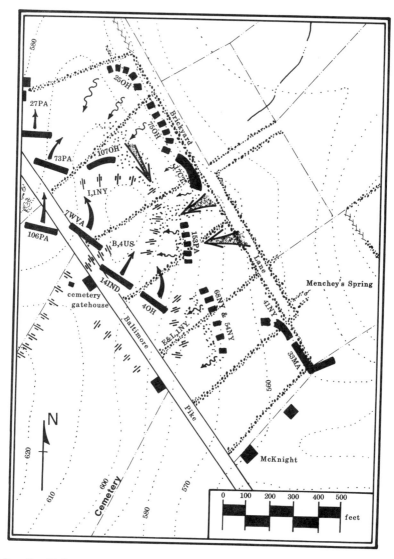

Map 5: Colonel Carroll's Brigade Arrives on East Cemetery Hill to a Scene "of Wildest Confusion"

Carroll's Men at Evergreen Cemetery Gatehouse

Edwin Forbes painting of Colonel Carroll's men approaching the Evergreen Cemetery Gate House. The Federal unit in the foreground may be the 14th Indiana which moved to the south of the gatehouse. In the distance (at the left middle of the field) Confederate troops work their way into Captain Ricketts' battery.

(*Library of Congress.*)

Evergreen Cemetery Gate

Colonel Carroll's men moved past the cemetery gate as they crossed the Baltimore Pike on which the horse and buggy stand, on their way toward Captain Ricketts' imperiled battery. The 14th Indiana and 4th Ohio charged around the gatehouse to its left, and the 7th West Virginia advanced on its right.

(*Library of Congress.*)

The 14th's color-bearer, Corporal Isaac Norris of Company H, was shot in the head and killed instantly; "other hands took up the colors and with loud cheers all along the line we went forward driving everything before us."[114] Another member of the regiment wrote that he and his comrades

> were made almost demons. Sharp, short and decisive in the gloom of night was this struggle, when the enemy broke and ran, we following stumbling in the dark over their dead and wounded.

The Rebels soon broke under the pressure of Coons' rush into the battery and ran "pell mell" down the east slope of Cemetery Hill.[115] The trailing Hoosiers captured a number of the 21st North Carolina, including its colonel, major, and battleflag.[116]

The 4th Ohio formed line of battle on the right of the 14th Indiana and a short distance south of the cemetery entrance. Private William Kepler remembered crossing the Baltimore Pike and then moving by the left flank up the slope of the hill "through tanglements of retreating men, caissons and horses, up and along a slope, where maddened gunners of

---

[114]David Beem, Speech, USAMHI; Beem, "History of the Fourteenth"; Captain Beem claimed that the 14th fired several volleys while in and around the battery before driving the Confederates down the hill.

That night, Corporal Norris was buried with several of his comrades, where they had fallen (Beem, "History of the Fourteenth").

[115]David Beem to Wife, July 5, 1863, USAMHI; *O.R.*, vol. 27, part 1, p. 459; "M," "What the 14th Ind. Did"; Caines, "A Gettysburg Diary"; Colonel Coons claimed that when he arrived at the battery, one of the rifles was in the possession of the Rebels. Coons also stated that his men drove the Rebels from a gun "they [the Rebels] had taken down the hill over a stone fence 100 yards in front of the battery." This is the only reference to an artillery piece actually being dragged away from a Federal battery on East Cemetery Hill although the most recent historian of the 14th Indiana suggested that the Rebels were preparing to remove some of the rifles from their positions near the top of the hill (Baxter, **Gallant Fourteenth**, p. 151).

[116]Charles H. Myerhoff, "What Troops did Carroll's Brigade Displace in the Charge," *National Tribune*, April 24, 1890; *O.R.*, vol. 27, part 1, p. 459.

General Hays' Confederates Attacking Ricketts' Battery

Pencil and wash drawing by Alfred R. Waud of Confederate troops of General Harry Hays' columns attacking Captain Ricketts' artillery position on East Cemetery Hill. The inscription on the back of the sketch reads: "The sketch represents it as too dark–Gettysburg–July 1-3-63-."

(*Library of Congress.*)

captured batteries raved and swore, or cried in very madness."[117] The cheering Ohioans stormed into the melee swirling about Ricketts' battery and with "bayonets and butts of guns at once joined the efforts of the heroic gunners."[118] After a brief hand-to-hand fight and "a few rounds," the 4th Ohio, with their comrades in the 14th Indiana, drove the Rebels out of the battery and down the hill, taking prisoners all the way.[119]

As they rushed across the Baltimore Pike, Carroll's left flank received scattered small arms fire from a number of Louisianians behind a stone wall. The colonel responded by ordering the 7th West Virginia, the left flank unit of his brigade, to change front so that it now faced north. This move prompted some of the graycoats to hastely abandon their shelter.[120] The West Virginians captured a number of the slower Rebels at the fence.[121]

---

[117]*Ibid.*, pp. 459, 460; Kepler, ***History of the Three Months***, p. 128; William Kepler heard an artilleryman shout, "It's Carroll's brigade, there'll be no more running; give 'em hell, boys" as the Buckeyes approached the battery.

[118]*Ibid.*, p. 129; Kepler made reference to Confederate soldiers preparing to remove some Federal artillery pieces.

[119]Silverman, "The Excitement Had Begun," p. 275; *O.R.*, vol. 27, part 1, p. 460; Kepler, ***History of the Three Months***, p. 129; Kepler claimed that the 5th Maine Battery was firing as Carroll's men forced the Southerners down the hill. This was echoed by a member of Captain Ricketts' battery (Sweet, "Ricketts's Battery").

[120]Coddington, ***Gettysburg Campaign***, p. 437; *O.R.*, vol. 27, part 1, p. 457; A member of the 14th Indiana ("M," "What the 14th Ind. Did") claimed that Colonel Coons ran up to the stone wall on Carroll's left and asked, "Who are you?" The men on the other side of the wall responded by stating that they were Union soldiers and then began firing. After this, the "Union" soldiers ran away with Coons "speeding his revolver bullets after them." Evidently the "Tigers" had tried a bit of deception on the Colonel Coons.

[121]*O.R.*, vol. 27, part 1, p. 463; In his post-battle report, Lieutenant Colonel Lockwood claimed that his men captured the colonel of the 7th Virginia. This regiment was not on East Cemetery Hill; Lockwood may have meant the 7th Louisiana of General Hays' brigade.

Private John T. Whitzal, Co. B, 7th West Virginia Infantry

One of roughly 230 West Virginians who charged to East Cemetery Hill on the evening of July 2, 1863.

(Jerry E. Rinker Collection, USAMHI.)

As soon as the Rebels were swept from the batteries on East Cemetery Hill, Federal artillerymen fired "deadly parting salutes" of double-shotted canister. Believing that the fighting was essentially finished, Colonel Wainwright ordered the artillery to cease fire so that the smoke hanging over the field might clear. At about this time, an officer approached the First Corps artillery commander requesting that he order his batteries to suspend their firing because Carroll's infantrymen were chasing the Rebels down the hill.[122]

While the 7th West Virginia focussed its attention on the Louisianians along the stone wall near the top of East Cemetery Hill, the 14th Indiana and 4th Ohio pursued the fleeing Confederates down the east face of the hill and beyond the stone fence at its base. Colonel Coons recalled that his men fired two or three volleys from behind the fence, after which the Confederates disappeared into the smokey night.[123]

Naturally the Confederates viewed their repulse from East Cemetery Hill somewhat differently than their counterparts in blue. General Jubal Early wrote that although his men had gained the batteries near the top of the hill, they were not supported on their right flank. Indeed, after gaining the batteries on the hill, General Hays observed an approaching line of infantry which began peppering his troops with minie balls. Unsure of the identity of these troops, Hays ordered his men to hold their fire (the brigadier had been cautioned to expect "friends both in front, to the right, and to the left, Lieutenant-General Longstreet, Major-General Rodes, and Major-General Johnson, respectively"). Hays quickly perceived the true nature of the situation when the unidentified line sent two volleyes into the "Tigers." The general ordered his men to retaliate in

---

[122]Moore, "Charge of the Louisianians"; Murdock, "On Cemetery Hill"; Nevins, A *Diary of Battle*, p. 246; Colonel Wainwright (*O.R.*, vol. 27, part 1, p. 358) wrote that the assault of East Cemetery Hill was "almost entirely repulsed by the artillery." On the other hand, Lieutenant George Breck (*Ibid.*, p. 363) of Battery L, First New York Light Artillery, just to the right and down the hill from Captain Ricketts' rifles, wrote that the Confederate assault "was mostly repelled by the infantry in support [Carroll's brigade]."

[123]"M," "What the 14th Ind. Did"; *O.R.*, vol. 27, part 1, p. 459; Coddington, *Gettysburg Campaign*, p. 438; Elijah Cavins of the 14th recollected that a "furious firing was continued by our troops for a short time after we arrived at the stone wall" (Caines, "A Gettysburg Diary").

kind but soon realized his command was surrounded. The Louisianians and North Carolinians began to fall back to the stone fence at the base of the hill "which was quietly and orderly effected." Hays realized that assistance would not be forthcoming and directed his men back to Confederate lines.[124]

In his official report, Colonel Archibald C. Godwin, temporary commander of Hoke's Brigade, wrote that his North Carolinians were not withdrawn until it became evident that "no supports were at hand." Major Samuel Tate, commander of the 6th North Carolina, declared that although a number of his men had successfully reached the batteries, it soon became painfully obvious that more men were needed. The Tarheels were forced down the hill after Tate was informed that support was not available. Describing his desperate plight on East Cemetery Hill, the major wrote:

> It was manifest that I could not hold the place without aid....Finding the enemy were moving up a line [Carroll's brigade], I ordered the small band of heroes to fall back from the crest to a stone wall on the side of the hill, where we awaited their coming. Soon they came over the hill in pursuit, when we again opened fire on them, and cleared the hill a second time....under cover of the darkness, I ordered the men to break and to risk the fire. We did so, and lost not a man in getting out.[125]

After pursuing the Southerners to and beyond the bottom of the hill, Colonel Coons reformed his regiment along the stone fence with the 7th West Virginia on his left flank and the 4th Ohio on the right.[126] As soon as they reached the stone wall, the 4th Ohio deployed skirmishers "well to their front" and brought in a number of Confederates. J.L.

---

[124]*O.R.*, vol. 27, part 2, pp. 470, 480-481; General Hays reported the capture of four stands of Federal colors.

[125]*Ibid.*, pp. 485, 486.

[126]*Ibid.*, part 1, p. 459; Elijah Cavins (Caines, "A Gettysburg Diary") believed that the 7th West Virginia remained farther up the east slope of Cemetery Hill facing north "until next morning."

Dickelman of the 4th recalled that when his regiment came upon the stone fence they were ordered to open fire on the fleeing Southerners. After firing "about 40 or 50 rounds," the Buckeyes were ordered to cease fire. Private Dickelman recalled a stranded Rebel in the dark field. The forlorn grayback, an "Irishman and brother," called out to the Yankees at the base of the hill, "Hould on, byes; I'm wan ov yoursilves. Don't shoot me!" The Southerner was ordered to approach and climb over the stone fence. As the grateful man obliged his captors, he exclaimed "Thank Jasus, I'm in the Union again!"[127]

Sporadic small arms fire continued until almost 10:30 p.m. after which skirmishers were deployed in the rolling fields beyond the Gibraltar Brigade's front. Skirmishers on the 4th Ohio's front rounded up numerous Rebels who had remained in the fields east of Cemetery Hill.[128] Although the firing on East Cemetery Hill had ended, "the terrible racket of musketry continued until near 11 o'clock" from Culp's Hill to the southeast.[129]

Finally finding time to search out his three regiments, Colonel Carroll discovered his men unsupported along the stone fence at the bottom of East Cemetery Hill. Though he wanted to pull his men back to the Second Corps line on Cemetery Ridge, both generals Howard and Ames requested that Carroll hold his men in position along the stone fence claiming that they were the "mainstay" of that part of the line. The colonel reluctantly agreed to remain in position.[130] Between 9:30 and 10:00 p.m. General Ames' troops began filing back into line on the left of Carroll's men.[131] Fearing another attack, Ames' strengthened his line by

---

[127]Dickelman, "Gen. Carroll's Gibraltar Brigade"; *O.R.*, vol. 27, part 1, p. 460; Major Allen G. Brady of the 17th Connecticut maintained that his regiment was relieved by the 4th Ohio (*Ibid.*, p. 718).

[128]Kepler, *History of the Three Months*, p. 129; *O.R.*, vol. 27, part 1, p. 457.

[129]Kepler, *History of the Three Months*, p. 129.

[130]Coddington, *Gettysburg Campaign*, p. 438 (fn. 135, p. 766); Colonel Carroll's three regiments remained in position at the base of East Cemetery Hill until July 5 (*O.R.*, vol. 27, part 1, p. 457).

[131]*Ibid.*; Coddington, *Gettysburg Campaign*, p. 438; General Howard wrote (*O.R.*, vol. 27, part 1, p. 706) that "the old position was resumed by regiments

placing the 106th Pennsylvania along the low stone fence on the left of Captain Weidrich's battery where the regiment would stay for the remainder of the battle.[132]

Carroll's men at the bottom of East Cemetery Hill surveyed the field in their front. A member of the 4th Ohio wrote in his diary that "the moon rose and shed its sickly light over the field. None of the enemy could be seen, except the dead and severely wounded."[133] At about 11:00 p.m. Companies G and I of the 4th Ohio were reunited with the rest of the regiment at the stone fence. The men of these companies and several members of the Pioneer Corps were detailed "to bring off their wounded, bury their dead comrades, and mark their graves."[134]

---

of my corps" at 9:30 p.m. Colonel Harris recalled that after the fighting ended his regiments "took up a position at the stone wall in the rear of, and parallel with the one occupied the previous day my left resting on the Baltimore Road." This stone fence is probably the one from which the 107th Ohio fought after falling back. The colonel went on to state that before daylight on July 3 he was ordered to move his men to the right along the stone fence. His deployment at that time had the 107th and 25th Ohio facing north on the left wing of the brigade; the right wing, the 75th Ohio and 17th Connecticut faced east along the stone fence at the base of East Cemetery Hill (Andrew L. Harris to John Bachelder, April 7, 1864, *in* Ladd and Ladd, ***Bachelder Papers***, 1: p. 139; Troop Position Map, July 3, 1863, *in Ibid.*).

[132]*Ibid.*, pp. 434, 706; Ward, ***One Hundred and Sixth Pennsylvania***, p. 163; The 106th Pennsylvania had arrived on East Cemetery Hill just as Colonel Carroll's men advanced into Captain Ricketts' battery.

[133]Silverman, "The Excitement Had Begun," p. 275.

[134]Kepler, ***History of the Three Months***, p. 130; Casualties suffered by Colonel Carroll's three regiments during their action on East Cemetery Hill are difficult to assess. Lemuel Jefferies of the 4th Ohio believed that his regiment lost 37 men killed and wounded during the repulse of the Confederates (Silverman, "The Excitement Had Begun," p. 275). Elijah Cavins of the 14th Indiana (Caines, "A Gettysburg Diary") recalled that his regiment lost six men killed in action and one mortally wounded as well as "quite a number wounded." The 14th Indiana lost 5 men killed and 3 mortally wounded at Gettysburg. All of them fell on July 2 (John W. Busey, ***These Honored Dead. The Union Casualties at Gettysburg*** (Hightstown, New Jersey: Longstreet House, 1988), p. 25). Eight men of the 4th Ohio were killed and 4 mortally wounded. However, ten of these men were members of Companies G and I, the

It had been a long day. For more than 19 hours, Colonel Carroll's men had marched, anticipated orders that seemed would never be issued, moved from one part of the line to another, withstood several artillery fusillades, and finally, almost thankfully, were thrown into a brief but confusing melee on East Cemetery Hill. Although their part in the fight had lasted only a short time, what one man recalled as "only a few minutes," Carroll's veterans believed that they had played an vital role in gaining a Federal victory at Gettysburg. However, others who had been on East Cemetery Hill that evening and night held different opinions.[135]

---

skirmish companies, which did not take part in the fighting on East Cemetery Hill. Thus the 4th lost a maximum of 2 men killed in the fighting on the evening of July 2 (*Ibid.*, p. 175). The 7th West Virginia suffered four men killed and 5 mortally wounded at Gettysburg. One of these men was on brigade provost guard duty during the battle (*Ibid*, p. 273).

[135]Caines, "A Gettysburg Diary"; One of Captain Ricketts' batterymen recollected that the attack and the fighting among the artillery pieces lasted about 30 minutes (Moore, "Charge of the Louisianians").

POST-BATTLE DEBATE: 1864

An honest, unemotional reading of the records reveals that the Federal line on East Cemetery Hill was, to a large extent, preserved by the combined efforts of Second and Eleventh Corps infantry as well as artillerymen of Captains Weidrich's and Ricketts' batteries. Nonetheless, a dispute pitting Colonel Carroll's Second Corps volunteers against the maligned Eleventh Corps veterans of General Ames' (Barlow's) division unfolded less than eight months after the battle. The debate, which would continue intermittently for 50 years, may have had its origins in General Howard's post-battle report submitted at the end of August 1863. Describing the Confederate assault of his line on the evening of July 2, the Eleventh Corps commander wrote:

> The attack was so sudden and violent that the infantry in front of Ames was giving way. In fact, at one moment the enemy had got within the batteries. A request for assistance had already gone to headquarters, so that promptly a brigade of the Second Corps, under Colonel Carroll, moved to Ames' right, deployed, and went into position just in time to check the enemy's advance. At Weidrich's battery, General Ames, by extraordinary exertions, arrested a panic, and the men with sponge staffs and bayonets forced the enemy back. At this time he received support from General Schurz. Effective resistance was also rendered at this time by a portion of General Steinwehr's command at points where the enemy was breaking through. This furious onset was met and withstood at every point, and lasted less than an hour. At 9:30 p.m. the old position was resumed by the regiments of my corps, Colonel Carroll remaining between Ames and Wadsworth. Lest another attack should be made, Ames' position was further strengthened by the One hundred and sixth Pennsylvania Regiment, from the Second Corps.[136]

---

[136] *O.R.*, vol. 27, part 1, p. 706.

Major General Oliver Otis Howard

Commanded the Eleventh Corps, Army of the Potomac at Gettysburg. His post-War writings of the fighting at Gettysburg and on East Cemetery Hill in particular infuriated veterans and partisans of the Second Corps.

(*Library of Congress.*)

A particularly interesting document relating to the debate is a short letter General Howard wrote to Colonel Carroll a month before the Eleventh Corps commander submitted his battle report and just 27 days after the fight on East Cemetery Hill. General Howard wrote:

> Colonel: I wish to thank you for the prompt support you gave me on the evening of July 2, at Gettysburg, on the extreme right of General Ames' division. I was particularly weak at that point, having only a single thin line, through which the enemy were just breaking. You came up quickly, deployed, and moved into position after your old style. For this and for your subsequent patience in strengthening that position until the close of the attack on July 3, I tender you my hearty thanks.[137]

Although Howard's motivation for this letter cannot be determined, it may have been an attempt to smooth over a small problem that developed when Carroll was asked to remain on East Cemetery Hill after the fighting had ended. Certainly the colonel's displeasure at having to linger on the Federal right was no secret. In fact, Carroll voiced his desire to be released to his Second Corps division several times on July 3.[138] On the other hand, Howard may have simply wished to thank a friend for providing help at a critical moment. The Eleventh Corps commander and Carroll had been close friends. The colonel and his family had shared a house with General Howard's family while both officers were at West Point.[139]

In any event, the Eleventh Corps underwent major changes in the few months following Gettysburg. On July 17, Brigadier General George H. Gordon was assigned to command of the First Division.[140] The new

---

[137]*Ibid.*, p. 711; General Howard's letter to Colonel Carroll was dated July 29, 1863, and written from Warrenton Junction, Virginia.

[138]Coddington, **Gettysburg Campaign**, p. 438.

[139]Pfanz, **Culp's Hill and Cemetery Hill**, p. 264.

[140]*O.R.*, vol. 27, part 3, p. 802; General Gordon's former command, the Second Division of the Fourth Corps, was incorporated into the First and Third Divisions of the Eleventh Corps.

division commander was not at all happy with his reassignment and on July 29, the brigadier penned a letter to General Howard regarding the proposed dismantling of the corps. Gordon maintained that the Eleventh Corps' poor reputation reflected "its disgraceful record at Chancellorsville and not a clean reputation at Gettysburg," as well as its inferior officers and general lack of discipline. This substandard reputation, Gordon continued, resulted in demoralization of the troops and rendered them "worthless while they wear its [the Eleventh Corps] badge." The newly appointed division commander added that the poor standing of the corps affected conscripts who entered by filling them "with dejection and indifference." Gordon finally got his wish to be rid of the Eleventh Corps when, in the middle of August, he and six regiments of the First Division were transferred to the Tenth Corps, Department of the South, stationed on Folly Island, South Carolina. Toward the end of September, the remainder of the Eleventh Corps, together with the Twelfth Corps, was transferred to Tennessee.[141]

The smoldering controversy between Colonel Carroll's men and the now departed Eleventh Corps was ignited on January 28, 1864, when the 38th Congress, after much behind-the-scenes politicking, passed a joint resolution of thanks to several officers and the men of the Army of the Potomac for the Federal victory at Gettysburg. Major General Hooker was credited with covering "Washington and Baltimore from the meditated blow of the advancing and powerful army of rebels." Cast in secondary roles, Major Generals George G. Meade and Oliver O. Howard "and the officers and soldiers" of the Army of the Potomac received plaudits "for the skill and heroic valor which at Gettysburg, repulsed, defeated, and drove back, broken and dispirited, beyond the Rappahannock, the veteran army of the rebellion."[142]

---

[141]*Ibid.*, pp. 778-779; *New York at Gettysburg*, 1: 307; Dyer, ***Compendium of the War***, 1: 318, 319, 320; All of the First Division regiments except the 153rd Pennsylvania and the 68th New York were part of the transfer. The 153rd was mustered out of the army at the end of July (***Pennsylvania at Gettysburg***, 2: 1143) and the 68th New York was temporarily transferred to the Second Brigade, Third Division, Eleventh Corps.

[142]*The Congressional Globe*, The Official Proceedings of Congress, 38th Congress, 1st Session, 1864, pp. 17, 421; On February 1, 1864 President Lincoln signed the resolution into law.

Although most people, civilian and military, agreed that the long-suffering eastern army was certainly due the thanks of the country for defeating General Lee's powerful army, some believed it inappropriate to single out General Howard from the other corps commanders for special recognition. One soldier who expressed very strong emotions along these lines was General John Gibbon, temporary Second Corps commander at Gettysburg. The former artilleryman "could see no propriety in connecting, even remotely, Hooker's name with the battle of Gettysburg and even less in selecting one of the corps commanders, and that one Gen. Howard." Gibbon declared that if Congress judged it necessary to acknowledge a corps commander, it should be General Hancock who, even though a junior to Howard, was ordered by General Meade to take command of the field on the afternoon of July 1.[143]

On February 20, 1864, the *Army and Navy Journal*, the "Gazette of the Regular and Volunteer Forces," included a response to the Congressional joint resolution of thanks. Echoing General Gibbon's sentiments, the author, who went by the pseudonym "Truth," questioned why General Howard was singled out for recognition while General Hancock, who "Truth" commended for his deft handling of a critical situation at Gettysburg on the afternoon of July 1, received no mention. "No man who witnessed the advent of General Hancock on this field will forget the almost magic change his arrival created," the author attested. Regarding the behavior exhibited by Howard's First Division troops on the evening of July 2, "Truth" insisted that the Eleventh Corps

> was not equal on that occasion to the task of driving back the enemy. The regiments from the Second Corps went forward with a run and retook the guns and position. General Howard has privately stated his opinion of the extreme value of this unexpected reinforcement.

The "private" statement referred to by "Truth" may have been Howard's July 29, 1863, letter to Colonel Carroll. In any event, the Second Corps partisan concluded his article by professing that General Hancock's

---

[143] Gibbon, *Personal Recollections*, p. 185.

Brigadier General John Gibbon

General Gibbon had temporary command of the Second Corps on the evening of July 2, 1863. In early 1864, Gibbon, who may have written under the pseudonym "Truth," expressed outrage over the special recognition conferred upon General Howard by Congress. He also voiced concern over the lack of "public and official acknowledgement" accorded Colonel Carroll and his men for their part in the fighting on East Cemetery Hill.

(*National Achives.*)

reputation is fixed on too substantial basis to be dependent on any action by Congress. The injustice lies in the fact that Congress has perpetuated what has always been a perversion of an impartial history of Gettysburgh [sic]; the statement that Major-General Howard was in any sense entitled to honors [is] not shared by other corps commanders."[144]

In addition to being distressed by the Congressional resolution, General Gibbon was concerned with "some facts coming out in regard" to role of Colonel Carroll's brigade on East Cemetery Hill. "It has recently come to my notice," wrote Gibbon to Carroll on February 23, "that you have failed to receive from Maj.-Gen. Howard the official acknowledgment to which you and your brigade are entitled by your services with his corps at Gettysburg on the night of the [July] 2d." The brigadier lamented this apparent oversight and stated that if he had been with the brigade, they would have received their just desserts. "Although I am told they were appreciated and acknowledged at the time [the evening of July 2]," Gibbon continued, "you failed to obtain that public and official acknowledgment which every soldier has the right to expect." As acting Second Corps commander on the evening of July 2, Gibbon felt it his duty to rectify this perceived error of omission. The general professed that he had no official knowledge of Carroll's "services whilst detached from the Second Corps," implying that he never saw a copy of Carroll's report submitted on July 5. In any event, Gibbon concluded his article by inviting Carroll to make whatever use of the February 23 letter that the colonel deemed proper in order to receive the "just acknowledgment" of his vital role at Gettysburg.[145]

---

[144]"Truth," "Congress and General Howard," *Army and Navy Journal*, February 10, 1864, p. 403.

[145]Gibbon, *Personal Recollections*, pp. 199-200; One must wonder if General Gibbon was aware of Howard's July 29 letter to Carroll. Gibbon may have been unfamiliar with Howard's battle report or, alternatively, was unhappy with the Eleventh Corps commander's statement that Carroll's men had arrived "just in time to check their [the Rebels] advance." Gibbon wrote his letter to Carroll from Philadelphia where, since November 1863, the general had been serving with the headquarters of the Draft Rendezvous. He was not reunited with the Army of the Potomac until late March 1864 (*Ibid*, pp. 184, 209).

On March 3, Colonel Carroll responded to General Gibbon. Carroll was particularly pleased with the general's commendations "after having been for so long a time officially ignored by the officer [General Howard] from whom we had a right to expect an acknowledgment of our services." One wonders why the colonel made no mention of Howard's July 29 letter. In any event, Carroll sought permission from Gibbon to publish Gibbon's February 23 letter "as a corroboration of the statement in the 'Army and Navy Journal,' dated Feb. 20th and signed 'Truth.'"[146] Thus, the controversy that derived from the inclusion of General Howard's name in the Congressional resolution of thanks was supplanted by a dispute between supporters of Colonel Carroll and his veterans and partisans of General Howard and the Eleventh Corps.

The March 12 issue of the *Army and Navy Journal* contained an article responding to "Truth's" February 20 piece.[147] The fact that this short piece included the text of General Gibbon's February 23 letter to Colonel Carroll suggests that the author, who used the pseudonym "Adjutant," was probably Carroll himself.[148] In addition to Gibbon's letter, "Adjutant" corrected "Truth's" statement regarding the number of Second Corps regiments sent to General Howard on the evening of July 2. The author also failed to point out the timely assistance rendered by Eleventh Corps troops.

> Three regiments of this brigade, under Col. Carroll's command, were first sent and some time afterwards two

---

[146]*Ibid.*, pp. 200-201.

[147]"Adjutant," "Congress and General Howard," *Army and Navy Journal*, March 12, 1864, p. 489.

[148]The identities of "Adjutant" and "Truth" remain baffling. Richard Sauers postulated that Colonel Carroll was "Truth" (Richard A. Sauers, *The Gettysburg Campaign, June 3-August 1* (Westport, Connecticut: Greenwood Press, 1982), p. 39). The fact that Carroll had informed Gibbon of his intention to submit a statement to the *Journal* that would basically confirm what "Truth" had claimed in the February 20 article also suggests that "Adjutant" was Colonel Carroll. Who, then, was "Truth"? A possible and even likely candidate is General Gibbon. The general's strong opinions regarding the Congressional resolution are essentially those expressed by "Truth."

more from the Second Division [of the Second Corps]. The latter two [71st and 106th Pennsylvania] did not come to the same part of the field as our brigade, which *alone* ("Adjutant's" emphasis) drove the enemy from Cemetery Hill.

One week later, another unidentified author known only as "One Who Knows" entered the controversy brewing in the pages of the *Army and Navy Journal*.[149] The author declared that his brief article was not offered in defense of Congress and the joint resolution, but rather to correct several statements made by "Truth." "One Who Knows" correctly pointed out that as the pressure of General Early's assault on Howard's line on the evening of July 2 mounted, the Eleventh Corps commander sent a request to General Meade for reinforcements. This call for help, the author continued, was then forwarded to General Gibbon who sent Colonel Carroll's brigade which ended up "on the right" of the Eleventh Corps line. The implications contained in "One Who Knows'" brief statement are meaningful. First, the author inferred that Carroll's men were sent to East Cemetery Hill because of General Howard's military acumen. Acceptance of this view would necessarily diminish General Hancock's role in helping to secure the Federal line on East Cemetery Hill. "One Who Knows" also insinuated that Carroll's regiments arrived *on* the right rather then *in support* of the Eleventh Corps line on East Cemetery Hill, a view that implied that General Ames' line was not breached. "One Who Knows" summed up by arguing that it was General Ames' men, augmented by some from General Steinwehr's division, who drove the Confederates off Cemetery Hill. Colonel Carroll's Second Corps volunteers arrived on the right just as the fighting was ending and, therefore, played no role in the Federal victory on East Cemetery Hill.

It is clear that by the end of March, General Howard had read the March 12 issue of *Army and Navy Journal* containing Gibbon's February 23 letter to Colonel Carroll. Howard appears to have decided to do what he could to correct the burgeoning misunderstanding. On March 27, the general sat down at his headquarters in Lookout Valley, Tennessee, and

---

[149]"One Who Knows," "Congress and General Howard," *Army and Navy Journal*, March 19, 1864, p. 499.

wrote the following letter to Army of the Potomac commander General Meade:

> Will you have the kindness to attach the inclosed copy of a letter written to Col. S.S. Carroll, commanding brigade, Second Corps, dated Warrenton Junction, Va., July 29, 1863, to my report of the battle of Gettysburg? Colonel Carroll never furnished me a report of the part taken by his command in that battle. I had presumed that he had done so to General Gibbon until I read General Gibbon's public letter complaining of my omissions. I will publish a card, with a view to setting the matter right.[150]

Howard's letter inferred that a break-down in communications had lead to the ill-feelings expressed in the *Army and Navy Journal* articles. Colonel Carroll's official report, dated July 5, was forwarded to Major J.M. Norvell, Third Division assistant adjutant general.[151] Three days later General Alexander Hays, commanding the Third Division, submitted his divisional report in which he commended Carroll for "the gallant manner in which they [Carroll's three regiments] went to the relief of the troops on the right."[152] On August 7 General Gibbon, recuperating away from the army in Baltimore, submitted his report which he claimed referred "partly to the Second Division and partly to the Second Corps." Gibbon pointed out that he had sent Carroll's brigade plus two other regiments to the assistance of the Eleventh Corps. One must wonder if Gibbon ever saw Carroll's report which described the July 2 actions of the Gibraltar Brigade. General Howard's post-battle report, so much desired by Gibbon, had been culled from division and brigade level reports and delivered to adjutant general Seth Williams, the person who should have received it after being endorsed by Meade. Gibbon was upset that he had never received a copy of the Eleventh Corps battle report describing Carroll's part in the action on East Cemetery Hill. Howard, however, was not obligated to submit a report to the acting Second Corps commander.

---

[150]*O.R.*, vol. 27, part 1, p. 711.

[151]*Ibid.*, pp. 457, 458.

[152]Dyer, *Compendium of the War*, 1: p. 287; *O.R.*, vol. 27, part 1, p. 453.

Nevertheless, it appears that the Eleventh Corps commander furnished this information to General Hancock who wrote in his Gettysburg battle report:

> I was gratified to hear subsequently, from General Howard in person, that it [Carroll's brigade] arrived at a very critical time, and that the unexpected re-enforcement materially assisted him in driving the enemy from his front.[153]

Hancock never expressed any dissatisfaction with the way Howard had described the action involving Colonel Carroll's brigade. Nevertheless, at the end of March, Howard, an honorable man, set out to see what he could do to rectify the problem.

The final shot in the debate carried out in the pages of the *Army and Navy Journal* was fired about one month before the Spring 1864 campaign commenced. The April 2 issue of the *Journal* included a second article by "Truth" who pointed out that Colonel Carroll's brigade was sent to the Federal right because General Hancock heard the sounds of fighting coming from that direction.[154] The author assailed "One Who Knows" for inferring that the Second Corps brigade was not needed because the Eleventh Corps soldiers had already repulsed the Confederates. "It is hardly generous now," proclaimed "Truth," "to create the impression that the Eleventh Corps was not in need of assistance but that it [according to "One Who Knows"] 'vigorously repulsed the enemy from its own front.'" Finally, "Truth" suggested that "If General Howard would permit what he had said to various people on the subject of Carroll's brigade to be made public there would be no more dispute on this point." Though he could not release his battle report to the public, Howard had already taken measures that he believed would set the record straight.

On the same day that he had written his note to George Meade, General Howard penned a letter or "card" to the editor of the *Washington*

---

[153] *O.R.*, vol. 27, part 1, pp. 372, 416-417.

[154] "Truth," "Congress and General Howard," *Army and Navy Journal*, April 2, 1864, p. 531.

Daily Chronicle.[155] Howard began his letter, published on April 5, by expressing "painful regret that I find it appearing that I have not complimented the gallantry and efficiency of Col. Carroll in such manner as was my purpose." The apologetic general insisted that his July 29, 1863, letter "was in no sense intended as a private letter." The text of this letter written so soon after the battle was included in the *Daily Chronicle* piece as proof of Howard's sincere gratitude to Carroll. The corps commander advised readers that he had recently requested that the letter be attached to the Eleventh Corps battle report, which Howard offered to have made public if possible (this was impossible at this time). Howard was surprised that General Gibbon was not aware of Carroll's actions on East Cemetery Hill. Attempting to clear the air and set the record straight, General Howard wrote:

> I warmly subscribe to the sentiment of Gen. Gibbon's letter [contained in "Adjutant's" March 12 *Army and Navy Journal* article] so far as it concerns Col. Carroll, and publicly disclaim any intention to do any injustice to him....I will add that I have omitted to commend several worthy officers who were connected with me and rendered the most honorable and timely service....[and]...I...am determined to make all possible amends for such omissions.

Near the end of his letter, Howard declared that Carroll's brigade "repulsed the enemy." The Eleventh Corps commander was forthright and willing to make amends even though, as he correctly implied, he was not completely at fault for the misunderstanding.

Publication of Howard's laudatory letter on April 5 should have assuaged the injured feelings of Colonel Carroll and Brigadier General Gibbon, and ended the controversy. Indeed, the Federal armies were preparing to move and all concerned parties had other things on their minds.

At 8:00 a.m. on May 4, 1864, Colonel Carroll's brigade, which now included the 14th Connecticut, 1st Delaware, 12th New Jersey, 10th New York Battalion and the 108th New York, in addition to the four

---

[155] Oliver O. Howard, *Washington Daily Chronicle*, April 5, 1864.

regiments that comprised the brigade at Gettysburg, crossed the Rapidan River and entered the Wilderness; the Spring Campaign of 1864 was underway. Late in the afternoon of May 6 General Longstreet's corps and part of Lieutenant General A.P. Hill's corps pushed east along the Orange Plank Road toward General Hancock's Second Corps line along the Brock Road. The Confederates struck Brigadier General Gershom Mott's division immediately south of the Brock Road-Orange Plank Road intersection. Some of the blue coats began to give way creating an opening in the line which Southern brigades commanded by Brigadier General Joseph R. Davis and Colonel John W. Henagan rushed to fill. Hancock recalled that "At the moment when the enemy reached our line, General Birney ordered Carroll's brigade, of Gibbon's division, to advance" against the Rebels climbing across the breastworks. The colonel's men, somewhat in the rear of the line, fixed bayonets and double-quicked by the left flank toward the breach in the line where, according to General Hancock, they forced "the enemy to fall back and abandon the attack in great disorder, with heavy loss in killed and wounded."[156] In a case of history repeating itself, Colonel Carroll's men had rushed to a threatened part of the Northern line and repulsed the enemy as they and others had claimed many of these same Second Corps veterans had done on East Cemetery Hill on the evening of July 2, 1863.

---

[156] *O.R.*, vol. 36, part 1, pp. 108, 324, 446, 447; Robert Garth Scott, ***Into the Wilderness with the Army of the Potomac*** (Bloomington, Indiana; Indiana University Press, revised and enlarged edition, 1992), pp. 167-168.

THE DEBATE IS RENEWED: 1876

When the fighting ended in spring 1865, the veterans returned home to pick up with their lives. Most of these men were more concerned with finding work and reacquainting themselves with family members and society in general than with refighting battles. The Confederate surrender found Colonel Carroll in command of a provisional division of the Army of the Shenandoah. Wounded on May 13 at Spotsylvania while in command of John Gibbon's division, Carroll did not return to duty until December. While convalescing, "Old Bricktop" was promoted to the rank of brigadier general to date from May 12, 1864. Carroll remained in the army after the war, spending two years as assistant inspector general of the Division of the Atlantic. By the middle of 1869, Major General Carroll's war wounds forced him to retire from the service.[157]

One former soldier who was concerned with how the fight on East Cemetery Hill might be presented by historians was Captain Ricketts. In early March 1866 he wrote to John Bachelder, the man charged with locating the positions occupied by the various regiments and batteries at Gettysburg, bemoaning the poor behavior of the Eleventh Corps on the evening of July 2. Ricketts sympathized with General Ames, who the former artillery officer incorrectly believed had the misfortune to "command a division of dutchmen." The captain characterized the conduct of the Eleventh Corps troops on his front, Colonel von Gilsa's men, when assailed by Confederate General Hays' Louisianians and North Carolinians as:

> cowardly and disgraceful in the extreme. As soon as the charge commenced, they, although they had a stone wall in their front, commenced running in the greatest confusion to the rear, hardly a shot was fired, certainly not a volley, and so panic stricken were they that several ran into canister fire of my guns and were knocked over.

---

[157]Warner, *Generals in Blue*, p. 73; Mark M. Boatner, III, *The Civil War Dictionary* (New York: David McKay Company, Inc., 1959), p. 129: Carroll, who had been breveted major general for war service, died on January 28, 1893.

Ricketts maintained that Colonel Carroll's brigade arrived at a most critical moment. "If I had received no support," the captain claimed, "my men would have been overpowered." According to Ricketts, Carroll's men deserved all of the credit for saving his battery as "none of the 11th Corps were rallied in time to assist in repulsing the charge." Unfortunately for General Howard's veterans, many Second Corps partisans accepted Ricketts' heavily biased version of the fighting on East Cemetery Hill.[158]

Seven years after Carroll retired from the army and twelve years after his supporters first voiced concern over what they perceived to be the former colonel's ill treatment at the hands of General Howard, the veterans renewed their feud, albeit for only a short time. As in 1864, Howard found himself at the center of the controversy. The occasion which upset some of the Second Corps veterans was publication of a lengthy article authored by Howard titled "Campaign and Battle of Gettysburg" in the July 1876 issue of the popular *Atlantic Monthly* magazine. Of the fighting on East Cemetery Hill, the former corps commander wrote:

> I sent to Meade for more troops, as a part of Ames's division was forced back and a gap made. But Hancock, hearing the firing, had detached Colonel S.S. Carroll, with his spirited brigade, to my aid. His men formed at right angles to the general line, and swept swiftly over the highest ground northward, carrying everything before them.[159]

Howard's article included two important corrections of his official report. First, he emphasized that Colonel Carroll's brigade had been dispatched to East Cemetery Hill because Hancock sensed trouble on that flank and not

---

[158] R. Bruce Ricketts to John Bachelder, March 2, 1866, *in* Ladd and Ladd, *Bachelder Papers*, 1: 235-236; Only Colonel von Gilsa's brigade comprised a majority of German soldiers. Captain Ricketts believed that the Confederate assault of Culp's Hill was only a diversionary action to draw troops from Cemetery Hill.

[159] Oliver O. Howard, "Campaign and Battle of Gettysburg," *Atlantic Monthly* 38 (July 1876): 65.

because of Howard's summons for help. Perhaps more important to many of the Second Corps veterans, however, was Howard's acknowledgment of the vital role that Carroll's brigade played in securing the right flank of the Eleventh Corps. In spite of these revisions to his earlier version of the events of the evening of July 2, Howard appears to have not been specific enough in his praise of Carroll's men for some of the more persnickety Second Corps partisans.[160]

Comments on Howard's article were quick in coming. The June 30, 1876, issue of the *Chicago Tribune* included a brief letter written by "Second Corps" outlining certain omissions from the *Atlantic Monthly* article. The July 2 issue of the *Tribune* contained a letter authored by a person simply known as "Carroll's Brigade."[161] The petty author complained that Howard had failed to point out that the artillery captured by the Louisiana "Tigers" on East Cemetery Hill belonged to Howard's own Eleventh Corps and, to make matters worse, the Eleventh Corps commander omitted this bit of information from his post-battle report. "Carroll's Brigade" went on to protest that Howard did not "officially acknowledge the services rendered him by Gen. Carroll" on the evening of July 2. One wonders exactly how Carroll's partisans would have worded the report describing the action of the Gibraltar Brigade on East Cemetery Hill. Finally, "Carroll's Brigade" crowed that Second Corps men saved *all* of the threatened artillery on East Cemetery. This statement was flatly incorrect; the author either ignored or was ignorant of the role that General Steinwehr's men and other Eleventh Corps troops played in recapturing Weidrich's battery.

---

[160]Howard never explained why he altered his view of the fighting on East Cemetery Hill expressed in the post-battle report. Either he did it simply to pacify certain vocal parties or he honestly believed the modifications to be true. Indeed, Howard had only Hancock's and Gibbon's versions of the orders that put Carroll's men in motion toward East Cemetery Hill. He probably realized that these officers would have had a better idea of what prompted Hancock (Gibbon) to send the Gibraltar Brigade toward the Federal right.

[161]"Second Corps," "Gen. Howard and Gettysburg," *Chicago Tribune*, June 30, 1876; "Carroll's Brigade," "Gen. Howard and Gettysburg," *Chicago Tribune*, July 2, 1876.

GENERAL HOWARD REKINDLES THE DEBATE: 1885

The nine years of apparent harmony between Second and Eleventh Corps partisans that endured after publication of the responses to former General Howard's *Atlantic Monthly* article ended on January 1, 1885, when his version of the fighting on East Cemetery Hill was published in the *National Tribune*, the principal newspaper of the Union veterans.[162] In this article, part of Howard's series titled "Personal Reminiscences of the War of the Rebellion," the former corps commander affirmed that the Louisiana "Tigers" broke through Colonel von Gilsa's line and other points along the Eleventh Corps front at the bottom of the hill. Shortly after getting in among Captain Weidrich's guns, the "Tigers" were cleared out by Eleventh Corps troops sent into the battery by General Schurz, as well as some of General Ames' rallied infantrymen. Even after this, Howard continued, "the broken lines were not yet restored." Discussing the movement of Colonel Carroll's brigade to the Eleventh Corps' right flank, Howard wrote:

> Gen. Hancock-not far off, not more than a quarter of a mile-"hearing a heavy engagement" on my front, and judging the firing to be coming nearer and nearer to his position, caused Gen. Gibbon to detach the brigade of Col. S.S. Carroll to my support.

After arriving on the scene, Carroll deployed his men in the darkness and, "with marvelous rapidity," swept everything in front of them helping to completely restore the line. Basically, Howard's *National Tribune* article reiterated much of what he had articulated in the *Atlantic Monthly* piece nine years before. And, like nine years before, Howard's writings provoked a heated response from Carroll's veterans and their allies.

The January 1, 1885 issue of the *National Tribune* also included an article by James Beale, a veteran of the 12th Massachusetts of

---

[162] O.O. Howard, "Personal Reminiscences of the War of the Rebellion; XLVII," *National Tribune*, January 1, 1885.

Brigadier General Henry Baxter's First Corps brigade.[163] Beale derided Howard's understanding of the fighting on July 1 and referred to the former Eleventh Corps commander's article as "altogether at variance with official papers, sworn statements and recorded history." Even after more than 20 years, the old Bay State volunteer was clearly distressed at the "very remembrance of a division of the Eleventh Corps throwing away its guns and manifesting intense anxiety to regain the charming shelter of Cemetery Hill." Beale's article, which was obviously written after he had had a chance to review Howard's "reminiscences" manuscript, also refuted the general's version of the events of July 2. Beale wrote that

> On July 2 his [Howard's] Eleventh Corps was still in nervous trepidation, for regiments had to be placed behind it with orders to fire on it; and when assailed by the Louisiana Tigers it fled pell-mell, Carroll's Brigade of the Second Corps being obliged to come to the rescue and retake the position.

Beale did not reveal the sources of his information regarding the actions of July 2. Baxter's brigade was in a reserve position behind the Evergreen Cemetery on that evening so that Beale did not have had a very good view of the fighting on East Cemetery Hill. Moreover, Comrade Beale's allusion to orders to shoot any Eleventh Corps men who broke out of line cannot be substantiated. Beale's comments regarding the action on East Cemetery Hill were clearly influenced by his jaundiced opinion of some units of Howard's Third Division which allegedly failed to support Baxter's right flank on July 1, 1863.

The January 22 issue of the *National Tribune* included another piece critical of General Howard's apparent misinterpretation of Colonel Carroll's important role on East Cemetery Hill. This article was authored by former Lieutenant John J. Reid, a member of the 8th Ohio who served on Colonel Carroll's staff at Gettysburg.[164] Reid asserted that Howard attempted to convey "the false impression that he did not call for any aid,

---

[163] James Beale, "Gettysburg, A Review of Gen. Howard's Account of the Battle," *National Tribune*, January 1, 1885.

[164] John G. Reid, "Gettysburg," *National Tribune*, January 22, 1885; *O.R.*, vol. 27, part 1, p. 458.

and that Carroll's Brigade was sent to him without solicitation." Ironically, in trying to champion Carroll's role in the action on East Cemetery Hill, Reid differed with what most Hancock and Second Corps devotees had claimed to be fact; that Howard's summons for help did *not* bring Carroll's men. Indeed, Howard had been assailed in 1864 for implying that his plea for assistance prompted Hancock to dispatch Carroll's brigade. Now the former Eleventh Corps commander was being maligned for asserting that Hancock had sent reinforcements without being ordered to do so. General Howard could not win for trying.

Reid continued his review of Howard's article by questioning the general's memory regarding the behavior of the Eleventh Corps troops at the base of East Cemetery Hill. The Buckeye declared that

> Howard has from the first been unwilling to admit that there was any actual break in his [Howard's] line on the evening of July 2...and hence he failed in his report, made within the next few days, to give Gen. Carroll and his Brigade the credit of saving same.

Even a casual reading of the pertinent sections of Howard's post-battle report as well as his ***Atlantic Monthly*** and ***National Tribune*** articles reveals that Reid was wrong. It appears that for the most part, Reid quarreled with Howard over trifling details rather than substantive matters.

In August 1885, the ***National Tribune*** published an article written by a former member of the 8th Ohio describing that regiment's operations at Gettysburg.[165] The September 10 issue included a similar article by a former member of the 14th Indiana. The Hoosier, however, wished to inform his readers of what Colonel Carroll's brigade did after the "glorious 8th Ohio" was deployed as skirmishers in the fields west of Cemetery Ridge.[166] Both veterans were more interested in recounting the movements and fighting of the brigade rather than becoming embroiled in

---

[165]"F," "Gettysburg."

[166]"M," "Gettysburg. What the 14th Ind. Did in the Fight"; "M" appears to have been Charles Myerhoff who became involved in the debate later in the century.

Charles H. Myerhoff

Charles H. Myerhoff, a member of the 14th Indiana, wrote about the East Cemetery Hill debate into the twentieth century. He appears to have published his first article in the *National Tribune* in 1885 under the pseudonym of "M."

a debate. John Reid's *National Tribune* article, then, concluded the second phase of the controversy.

In the early and middle 1880s, survivors' associations of various regiments and batteries which had fought at Gettysburg began publishing their unit histories. That of the 33rd Massachusetts, written by former Colonel Adin B. Underwood, was published in 1881. Recalling the evening of July 2, 1863, Underwood wrote that the Rebels broke "through and scattered some of the German regiments, in the Eleventh Corps on the slope" and took the artillery on the hill. Just when it appeared that the fragile line would collapse back to the Baltimore Pike and into the cemetery beyond, a combined thrust by several Eleventh Corps regiments on the left and Colonel Carroll's brigade on the right repulsed the Southerners and saved the artillery.[167] Underwood's impressions of this fighting mirrored those of Carroll as well as Howard.

Colonel Underwood's clear-eyed description of the fight on East Cemetery Hill was somewhat tarnished by his reference to the "German regiments" that he claimed broke during the Rebel assault. One must wonder how much anti-German sentiment entered into the feud between the Second and Eleventh Corps veterans. It was widely known that many officers of the Army of the Potomac, especially those American-born men of English ancestry, held a very low opinion of German soldiers. Much of this sentiment came to a head when the Eleventh Corps was crushed at Chancellorsville. Brigadier General Francis C. Barlow, for example, attributed the poor behavior of the corps at Chancellorsville to the German regiments, which actually constituted less than half the total corps strength. Barlow scornfully declared that although the Germans marched well enough, they were substandard fighters.[168] This example is

---

[167] Underwood, *Three Years Service*, pp. 130-131.

[168] Coddington, *Gettysburg Campaign*, p. 305; Other examples of the strong anti-German bias among many officers of the Army of the Potomac, especially those of New England Yankee heritage, can be found in the writings of Major Henry Livermore Abbott of the 20th Massachusetts (Robert Garth Scott, editor, ***Fallen Leaves. The Civil War Letters of Major Henry Livermore Abbott*** (Kent, Ohio: The Kent State University Press, 1991), pp. 92, 181). Referring to a fellow officer in the 20th, Abbott wrote that "he has also strong common sense, very good taste, considerable humor, & whenever he has a mind to throw off the heavy German air of stupidity, he can be one of the pleasantest men I

Colonel Adin B. Underwood

Commanded the 33rd Massachusetts Infantry at Gettysburg. Underwood authored the 33rd's history and claimed that the "German regiments" crumbled on the evening of July 2, 1863. Image taken when Underwood was a captain in the 2nd Massachusetts Infantry.

(*USAMHI.*)

---

ever met." In the middle of May 1863, Livermore penned a letter to his father recounting the fighting at Chancellorsville and made it a point to mention the "disgraceful flight of those miserable Dutchmen, who every body knew would run away."

particularly significant in that before he was injured on July 1, Barlow commanded the First Division which included Colonel von Gilsa's and General Harris' brigades, the commands which held the Federal line on East Cemetery Hill. In any event, as the Army of the Potomac recovered from Chancellorsville and finally began moving north toward Gettysburg, some in the Northern press suggested that the entire Eleventh Corps should be shot. In short, many people, in and out of the army, regarded the Germans as a low-class, pernicious group of people.[169] Certainly it is possible, then, that the strong feelings expressed by some former members of the Second Corps toward General Howard's veterans found their origins in the pervasive prejudice of German soldiers that existed during and even after the war.

The regimental history of the 25th Ohio was published in 1885. The right flank of this Buckeye regiment was uncovered when the 17th Connecticut was shifted to the right moments before the Louisiana "Tigers" struck the Federal line at the base of East Cemetery Hill. The author, Edward C. Culp, a former member of the 25th Ohio who had served on General Ames' staff, recalled that his brigade was quickly driven back to Captain Weidrich's battery. The men were rallied, however, and cooperated with the artillerymen to battle the Rebels among the rifles. Culp declared that Colonel Carroll's brigade "came to Ames' relief, and the enemy finding they were about to be overwhelmed, retreated in confusion."[170]

The following year, The Count of Paris, a former member of General McClellan's staff, published his history of the battle of Gettysburg. Writing of the fighting on East Cemetery Hill, The Count stated that General Hancock dispatched help to General Howard's beleaguered line when the Second Corps commander heard the sounds of

---

[169]Ella Lonn, *Foreigners in the Union Army and Navy* (Baton Rouge, Louisiana: Louisiana State University Press, 1951), pp. 594-595; The strong tone of the anti-German sentiment that became so obvious after Chancellorsville affected Germans to such an extent that they never expressed as a high degree of enthusiasm for the continuance of the war as they had before spring 1863.

[170]Edward C. Culp, *The Twenty-Fifth Ohio Veteran Volunteer Infantry in the War for the Union* (Topeka, Kansas: George W. Crane & Company, Printers, 1885), p. 79.

fighting on the Federal right. The French nobleman went on to explain that Colonel Carroll's men arrived "just at the moment when the issue of the desperate struggle that is going on around the guns seems exceedingly doubtful."[171] Thus it appears that contemporary historians, even those affiliated with the Eleventh Corps such as Edward C. Culp, resolved that Colonel Carroll's brigade, along with various regiments from the Eleventh Corps, was instrumental in defending the batteries on East Cemetery Hill. This should have satisfied both parties to the debate but, as might be expected with disputes involving the honor of aging veterans, it did not.

---

[171]Louis Philippe Albert d'Orleans, Comte de Paris, *History of the Civil War in America* 4 volumes, translated by Louis F. Tasistro. Volumes 1 and 2 edited by Henry Coppee. Volumes 3 and 4 edited by John P. Nicholson (Philadelphia: Porter & Coates, 1875-1888), 3: 188.

"THE CANNONEER" ADDS FUEL TO THE FIRE: 1889

Toward the end of 1889, more than four years after publication of former-lieutenant John Reid's biting review of General Howard's *National Tribune* piece, the *Tribune* began what would become a popular series of articles titled "The Story of a Cannoneer" by Augutus Buell.[172] Records indicate that Buell, a member of Battery B, 4th United States Artillery, did not enlist until August 21, 1863 so he could not have been at Gettysburg.[173] Recently, Buell's description of the actions he allegedly witnessed at Gettysburg was interpreted to be a transcription of oral history provided by a soldier of the 7th Wisconsin and two members of Battery B.[174] Nevertheless, the veterans *believed* that Buell was a witness to the fighting on East Cemetery Hill. "The Cannoneer's" articles would trigger the third period of debate concerning this action.

Augustus Buell's article on the fighting on July 2 appeared in the November 7, 1889, issue of the *Tribune*.[175] Describing the evening assault on the Eleventh Corps line, Buell wrote that Howard's men were swept away "like dust before a new broom." "The Cannoneer" asserted that the rout of von Gilsa's brigade uncovered Ames' (Colonel Harris') left flank causing that brigade to "break." As the situation became critical, Buell related that

---

[172] Silas Felton, "Pursuing the Elusive 'Cannoneer,'" *Gettysburg Magazine* #9 (July 1993): 33, fn. 2; Augustus Buell's series in the *National Tribune* began on October 10, 1889, and concluded with the April 3, 1890, issue. Three additional articles were published on May 15, May 22, and June 12, 1890.

[173] Milton W. Hamilton, "Augustus C. Buell, Fraudulent Historian," *Pennsylvania Magazine of History and Biography* 80 (October 1956): pp. 478-492.

[174] Felton, "Pursuing the Elusive 'Cannoneer,'" p. 39; Felton suggests that although Buell was not at Gettysburg, his account compares well with what many participants have described of the fighting involving the First Corps.

[175] Augustus Buell, "Story of a Cannoneer. Battle of Gettysburg," *National Tribune*, November 7, 1889.

Augustus Buell, "The Cannoneer"

Sketched from a war-time ambrotype.

(*Buell, The Cannoneer.*)

we heard cheers immediately on our right, and in a few
seconds a splendid brigade of our infantry swept past us
and charged straight at the ravine and wall, from which
they routed the rebels pell-mell, driving them clear to the
bottom of the hill and retaking Weidrick's [sic] and
Ricketts's guns.

Buell later learned that this "splendid brigade" was Colonel Carroll's three regiments.

Augustus Buell's articles on Gettysburg elicited a great number of responses. The November 28 issue of the *Tribune* contained a brief rejoinder by William Houghton, a former commissioned officer in the 14th Indiana.[176] The Hoosier officer complimented Buell "on his splendid memory and accurate detail of the second day at Gettysburg." After recounting Carroll's actions on the evening of July 2, Houghton concluded his article by declaring that the Second Corps brigade "saved the center and steadied the uncertain troops of the Eleventh Corps." This could not have set well with many of General Howard's veterans, especially those of the First Division.

The November 28 issue of the *National Tribune* also included article VIII in "The Cannoneer" series.[177] Buell devoted a good part of this piece to a discussion of the conduct of the Eleventh Corps at Chancellorsville and Gettysburg. The author noted that his comments regarding this corps which Buell incorrectly believed was composed predominantly of Germans, carried "no particular reflection on that nationality." Evidently Buell was aware of, and sensitive (in his own way) to the strong anti-German sentiment that existed within the Army of the Potomac. Nonetheless, the former artilleryman alleged that at Gettysburg, unlike at Chancellorsville, the Eleventh Corps was

neither surprised nor routed, [but] it was beaten and
driven back with ease, when compared with the terrible
slugging which was necessary to make the old First

---

[176] William Houghton, "Carroll's Brigade at Gettysburg," *National Tribune*, November 28, 1889.

[177] August Buell, "Story of a Cannoneer. The Eleventh Corps at Chancellorsville and Gettysburg," *National Tribune*, November 28, 1889.

William Houghton

A member of the 14th Indiana, Houghton believed that Colonel Carroll's brigade "steadied the uncertain troops of the Eleventh Corps" on the evening of July 2, 1863.

Corps let go of its position as the left wing of the army that day. On the second day of Gettysburg, just at sundown, the Eleventh Corps was again assailed in its new position, and this time its two advance brigades [von Gilsa's and Harris'] were fairly routed and driven up the steep hill about as fast as men are usually expected to run down hill.

However, Buell continued, there "was no disposition among the fighting veterans of the Old First [Corps] to join in the popular cry to 'D--n the Dutch.'

"The Cannoneer" attempted to deflect the ire of Eleventh Corps veterans by claiming that these men had done as good as could be expected given the crop of commanders they had to fight under. Division commanders such as Schurz and Steinwehr, Buell argued, were "amateurs or adventurers."[178] Buell went on to accuse brigade commanders such as von Gilsa, Coster, Cantador, von Amsberg and Kryzanowski of being nothing more than "foreign adventurers" who could not speak a word of English. In spite of this, "there was nothing wrong with the rank and file of the German regiments," confirmed Buell. In an attempt to demonstrate that most other veterans held no ill feelings toward the Eleventh Corps rank-and-file, Buell recalled a discussion he had had with a First Corps soldier shortly after Gettysburg. This man professed that the

> poor Dutch, though brave enough, are slow to anger, besides being a little dull, and so, probably they couldn't see that they were being "bilked" by their officers till it was too late, and they were all getting butchered.

This faint praise probably ended up alienating many Eleventh Corps veterans, especially the Germans.

The December 5, 1889, issue of the *National Tribune* included a brief response to Buell's November 7 article relating the fight on East

---

[178]Buell claimed that "the only real soldier among them" was Brigadier General Francis Barlow, a man who, as previously noted, felt nothing but scorn toward the Germans under his command.

Cemetery Hill by J.R. McClure, a prior member of the 14th Indiana.[179] The Hoosier complimented Buell for giving the *Tribune* readership the "straight goods" and recognizing Colonel Carroll for his vital role in securing the Federal line on East Cemetery Hill. Interestingly, McClure declared that Carroll "was the most abused man in the army." Unfortunately, he offered no explanation for this interesting statement.[180]

Five weeks after publication of Buell's account of the fighting on the Federal right flank, the *National Tribune* carried an article written by former First Lieutenant A.W. Peck of the 17th Connecticut, a man who would become the most prolific partisan of the Eleventh Corps defenders of East Cemetery Hill.[181] Though much of Comrade Peck's article addressed Buell's version of events involving the First and Eleventh Corps on July 1, he did touch on the part that the 17th Connecticut played in the fighting on the evening of July 2. Peck held that the 17th never fell back from the stone fence at the base of East Cemetery Hill, a claim that most honest participants in the fighting on that day had no quarrel with. However, Peck's credibility slipped a notch when, in a feeble attempt to prove that the infantry line at the base of the hill was never breached, he argued that that Ricketts' and Weidrich's batteries were never endangered because they were still on East Cemetery Hill on the morning of July 3. The former officer appears to have forgotten that these batteries were threatened and possibly in enemy hands for a short time. Some participants even implied that some of Ricketts' pieces were about to be carried off just as Carroll's men arrived on the scene.

---

[179] J.R. McClure, "Old Bricktop."

[180] On March 25, 1864 Captain James F. Huntington wrote the following to General Gibbon: "In the matter of promotion, I consider him [Colonel Carroll] the worst used man in the United States Army" (quoted in Reid, "What Our Veterans Have to Say"). Likewise, Dunn Browne of the 14th Connecticut wrote that Carroll's recommendations for promotion were turned down for lack of political influence until General Grant became General in Chief. Browne claimed that Carroll had been designated for promotion to general two or three times, but not confirmed because he lacked political influence (Fiske, *Mr. Dunn Browne's Experiences*, pp. 195-196).

[181] A.W. Peck, "Gettysburg. The Part Taken by the Eleventh Corps," *National Tribune*, December 12, 1889.

Two weeks later Augustus Buell responded to Comrade Peck by publishing a "Note" in the *Tribune*.[182] "It grieves me to see that my comments on the behavior of the [Eleventh] corps have been apparently misinterpreted," wrote Buell. "The Cannoneer" reiterated his claim that the problems with the corps stemmed from its officers. Buell maintained that if the various divisions and brigades had been commanded by such men as Reynolds, Sedgwick, Carroll and Webb, the Eleventh Corps would have performed much better. Betraying a certain degree of anti-German sentiment, Buell proposed that grouping men in regiments or batteries by nationality "is contrary to the American idea." Publication of Augustus Buell's "Note" in late December 1889 terminated the debate for a short time. The March 13, 1890, issue of the *Tribune*, however, contained a response to Lieutenant Peck's December 12 article authored by James Beale, formerly of the 12th Massachusetts.[183] Citing numerous passages from the ***Official Records***, Beale pointed out the obvious - that Peck was incorrect in relating that none of the artillery pieces on East Cemetery Hill were captured.[184] Beale also referred his readers to General Howard's report and July 29, 1863, letter to Colonel Carroll as evidence that *all* of the Eleventh Corps troops fell back from the stone fence at the base of the hill. The Bay Stater then focussed his discussion on two monuments on East Cemetery Hill as symbols of the relative roles of the Second and Eleventh Corps troops who fought there:

> If Lieut. Peck will visit the spot he will find on East Cemetery Hill, not far from an Eleventh Corps monument, (which, I think, is for Lieut. Peck's regiment,) a stone erected by a Second Corps regiment, on which is inscribed a quotation from Gen. Howard "You can take your guns away when this regiment leaves"-the history of

---

[182] Augustus Buell, "Note," *National Tribune*, December 26, 1889.

[183] James Beale, "Gettysburg. Some Facts for the Eleventh Corps to Digest," *National Tribune*, March 13, 1890; Recall that James Beale rebutted General Howard's January 1, 1885, *National Tribune* article on Gettysburg.

[184] Comrade Beale made reference to Captain Ricketts' and Brigadier General Robert O. Tyler's post-battle reports.

which may shed some light on Lieut. Peck's perplexity as to what happened there in the evening of July 2, 1863.

The "stone" Beale spoke of is a small marker erected by survivors of the 106th Pennsylvania in the mid-1880s (Refer to Appendix A for photographs of the 106th Pennsylvania's marker and the 17th Connecticut's monument).[185] The "history" of this marker was recounted at the dedication of the 106th's monument on Cemetery Ridge in September 1889. The speaker, James C. Lynch, related that as General Howard rode his line on the evening of July 2, he turned to his artillery chief Major Thomas W. Osborn and reportedly uttered the words inscribed on the monument.[186] Although Beale never really made his point, he appears to have implied that Howard felt safer with Second Corps troops in his line rather than Eleventh Corps men, and when things got so bad that the 106th Pennsylvania had to fall back, it would be time for everybody to leave.

Roughly half of Beale's article was a general attack on the Eleventh Corps. Derisively stating that "something must have been wrong" with the corps, Comrade Beale cited several comments made by various Eleventh Corps brigade and division officers regarding the proposed dismantling of the corps after Gettysburg. The author made reference to a letter written by Howard to General in Chief Henry Halleck on July 29, 1863, in which the corps commander approved of integrating two of his divisions into the Second and Twelfth Corps. What Beale failed to mention was that Howard

> hope[d] the changes referred to [would] not be regarded

---

[185] The small marker, located approximately 100 yards due west and upslope from the 17th Connecticut's monument along modern Wainwright Avenue, was erected sometime between 1884 and 1886 (Kathy Georg Harrison, *The Location of the Monuments, Markers, and Tablets on Gettysburg Battlefield* (Gettysburg, Pennsylvania: Thomas Publications, 1993), p. 14). The exact quotation on the monument is: "'Your Batteries Can Be Withdrawn When That Regiment Runs Away' Gnl. O.O. Howard to Maj. Osborn."

[186] *Pennsylvania at Gettysburg*, 1: 551; Lynch maintained that Howard's confidence in the 106th derived from the general's observations, as an officer in the Second Corps, of the regiment at Antietam and Fredericksburg.

Major Thomas W. Osborn

Commanded the Eleventh Corps Artillery Brigade at Gettysburg. The 106th Pennsylvania's marker on East Cemetery Hill contains an inscription of General Howard's alleged instructions to Osborn that the major's batteries should remain in position only until the 106th is forced to withdraw.

(*MOLLUS Collection, USAMHI.*)

> as a reflection upon the officers and soldiers of this command, who have worked so hard and done so much to carry out every order.[187]

Thus Howard believed that the problems with the Eleventh Corps sprang from other peoples' biased perceptions of his command rather than some organic troubles.

Beale cited a comment written by Colonel Adolphus Buschbeck to General von Steinwehr on July 30, 1863, in which the former asserted that "consolidation of this corps with some other corps would be in the interest of the service." Again, Beale conveniently failed to mention that Buschbeck was writing about the debacle at Chancellorsville and the "prejudice" cast over the Eleventh Corps since that defeat. The colonel continued:

> The officers and men of my brigade on that day [May 2, 1863] behaved with great bravery...and have always done their duty, yet they also suffer under this prejudice. It is, therefore, my opinion that consolidation of this corps with some other corps would be in the interest of the service.

Nonetheless, Buschbeck hoped that his brigade would remain in von Steinwehr's division, and that the division would continue to be a part of the corps commanded by General Howard. In sum, although Buschbeck believed that the Eleventh Corps should be broken up, he wished to remain a part of it.[188]

Beale quoted from a letter penned by Colonel Orland Smith to von Steinwehr at the end of July pronouncing that the reputation of the Eleventh Corps had been disgraced. Again, Beale failed to place the comment in the context of the complete letter. Smith wrote:

> Since the unfortunate affair near Chancellorsville, it is undeniable that the reputation of the corps has been such as to involve in reproach and mortification all parties

---

[187] *O.R.*, vol. 27, part 3, p. 778.

[188] *Ibid.*, p. 785.

> connected with it....Believing that many unjust aspersions have been cast, not only upon innocent members, but upon the whole corps, and that it will continue to be the butt of ridicule for irresponsible newspaper correspondents, and the scapegoat, perhaps, for all reverses, I am convinced that a change in organization would be of very great advantage, and promote in a high degree the good of the service. Such a consummation would dispel the despondency and discouragement which are unmistakably manifest in those whose patriotism is unquestioned, but whose reputation is dear to them, dearer, even, than life.

Colonel Smith concluded his letter by stating that "while a change of corps relations is desirable," he would like Howard to remain as corps commander and that his, von Steinwehr's, division remain intact.[189]

Finally, Comrade Beale discussed a particularly damning statement regarding the Eleventh Corps made by Brigadier General George H. Gordon, an officer Beale described as Lieutenant Peck's division commander. What Beale failed to point out was that Gordon had been assigned to command of the First Division of the Eleventh Corps in the middle of July.[190] Gordon's displeasure at his new command was obvious in his correspondence with General Howard. The brigadier felt that the only way to save the men of the Eleventh Corps from certain disaster was the break it up and dismiss the "worthless" officers. He seemed to echo Augustus Buell's claim that that the problems of the Eleventh Corps were rooted in its officers. In any event, Gordon wished to be reassigned to the Twelfth Corps where he would be reunited with his old regiment, the 2nd Massachusetts. As noted earlier, the new division commander's wish was granted although he was not reunited with his old command.[191] One might speculate how much of the Massachusetts-born

---

[189]*Ibid.*, pp. 785-786.

[190]*Ibid.*, p. 802; General Gordon's former command, the Second Division of the Fourth Corps, was incorporated into the First and Third Divisions of the Eleventh Corps.

[191]*Ibid.*, pp. 778-779.

brigadier general's resentment of the Eleventh Corps was colored by his New England Yankee upbringing and second-hand information.[192] In any event, Beale had been disingenuous about the context within which many of his cited comments had been made. Indeed, this would not be last time that Beale misrepresented or improperly used the *Official Records* to make a point.

In early April 1890 the *National Tribune* published a brief response to Augustus Buell's November 28, 1889, article on the Eleventh Corps at Chancellorsville and Gettysburg. The author, Louis Fischer, a former lieutenant in Company K, 74th Pennsylvania, agreed with "The Cannoneer's" thesis regarding the poor leadership of the Eleventh Corps. Fischer was particularly pleased with Buell's

> defense of the rank and file of a body of naturally brave men, who had been malignantly unfortunate from the very first in their brigade, division and corps commanders, with perhaps two or three exceptions-Sigel, Barlow and Schimmelfennig.[193]

Fischer concluded that, "It seemed to me that the Eleventh Corps existed only to be hurled into battle and then abandoned to its fate."

Comrade Peck's second response to Augustus Buell was published in the April 10, 1890, issue of the *National Tribune*.[194] He questioned several comments made by Buell in the December 26, 1889, "Note." Peck then introduced a new twist to the controversy by claiming that the Eleventh Corps units on East Cemetery Hill collapsed because that part of the line had been weakened by the removal of several regiments only a short time before the attack. As evidence, Peck cited an

---

[192] Warner, *Generals in Blue*, p. 177.

[193] Louis Fischer, *National Tribune*, April 3, 1890; The 74th Pennsylvania was part of Colonel George von Amsberg's First Brigade of Brigadier General Alexander Schimmelfennig's Third Division, Eleventh Corps. According to General Schurz, the 74th Pennsylvania was "left with General Ames to strengthen his right wing" when the balance of the brigade was sent to the sounds of fighting on Culp's Hill (*O.R.*, vol. 27, part 1, p. 731).

[194] A.W. Peck, *National Tribune*, April 10, 1890.

article published four years earlier in *The Century Magazine*. The author of this article, none other than Henry Hunt, former Chief of Artillery of the Army of the Potomac, wrote that the Eleventh Corps line at the base of East Cemetery Hill "had been weakened to send supports both the Greene [Brigadier General George S. Greene, commanding Third Brigade, Second Division, Twelfth Corps] and Sickles."[195] Peck recorded that it was "no wonder that the rebels broke through that part of the line, when a whole brigade had been taken away to support some other point." The former lieutenant's argument, that the East Cemetery Hill line was made vulnerable by the removal of a brigade just before General Hays' Louisianians and North Carolinians attacked, was simply not true. A review of the *Official Records* illustrates how Hunt and later Peck misinterpreted what really happened.

When the fighting on Culp's Hill began, Brigadier General Greene, whose brigade was the only Federal force holding the east face of the hill, sent urgent requests to General Wadsworth, on his immediate left, and General Howard for assistance.[196] Shortly before sending the 58th and 119th New York to Captain Weidrich's support, Howard ordered General Schurz to dispatch help to General Ames on East Cemetery Hill. The 74th Pennsylvania of Colonel von Amsberg's brigade was sent to Ames' assistance while the remaining four regiments of the brigade, the 157th and 45th New York, 82nd Illinois and 61st Ohio, were directed to

---

[195]Henry J. Hunt, "The Second Day at Gettysburg," *The Century Magazine* 23 (December 1886): 295; General Hunt also pointed out that the Eleventh Corps line was secured by the timely arrival of Colonel Carroll's regiments, which had been sent voluntarily by General Hancock. Lieutenant Peck conveniently failed to refer to this part of Hunt's narrative.

[196]*O.R.*, vol. 27, part 1, p. 856; Between 5:00 and 6:00 p.m. Brigadier General Alpheus Williams, temporary commander of the Twelfth Corps, was ordered by Major General Slocum to send Brigadier General Ruger's division and Brigadier General Henry H. Lockwood's unassigned brigade to the threatened left wing of the Army of the Potomac. Shortly after dark, Brigadier General John Geary's division, minus General Greene's brigade, vacated its breastworks and trenches on Culp's Hill to follow Ruger and Lockwood. This left only Greene's men to hold the line along Culp's Hill (*Ibid.*, pp. 774-775).

report to General Greene on Culp's Hill.[197] There is absolutely no evidence that any of Ames' regiments had been sent away from East Cemetery Hill; Peck was just wrong.

Finally, Comrade Peck questioned "The Cannoneer's" implication that demoralization of the Eleventh Corps was caused by its poor crop of officers. Peck proclaimed that "it is very evident that Howard was satisfied with his officers and men, or we who were right there would have heard something about it." While this may true, one must wonder if Peck knew anything about the discussions among various Eleventh Corps officers regarding the proposed dismantling of the corps not more than one month after the battle.

The April 24 issue of the *National Tribune* included a response to Comrade Peck's article by Charles Myerhoff, formerly of the 14th Indiana.[198] Myerhoff reiterated much of what he wrote several years prior about the fighting as he observed it on East Cemetery Hill.[199] The Hoosier was a bit miffed at Peck's claim that he never saw any of Colonel Carroll's men along the stone fence at the base of the hill. Myerhoff went to great lengths to describe that part of the line held by his regiment on the night of July 2 and the next day. Specifically, he recounted several incidents along the line that Peck should have remembered if, indeed, the Nutmeg officer had been there himself. Myerhoff then called upon Carroll himself to add what he knew of his brigades' position along the stone fence. Comrade Myerhoff ended his article by requesting that the veterans "be respectful of each other, and believe as much as we can that all tried to do their duty."[200]

---

[197] *Ibid.*, pp. 730-731; General Greene wrote that only the 45th New York and the 61st Ohio reached his position although the other two regiments were there (*Ibid.*, p. 856).

[198] Charles H. Myerhoff, "At Gettysburg," *National Tribune*, April 24, 1890.

[199] Charles Myerhoff appears to have been the author of a *National Tribune* article published in 1885 under the pseudonym "M" that described the 14th Indiana's part in the fighting at Gettysburg ("M," "What the 14th Ind. Did").

[200] In 1890 Augustus Buell's *National Tribune* articles were published in book form (Augustus Buell, *The Cannoneer. Recollections of Service in the Army of the Potomac* (Washington, D.C.: The National Tribune, 1890)). Buell recanted his opinion of the behavior of General Harris' brigade spelled

After a year of silence James Beale responded to A.W. Peck's April 10, 1890, *National Tribune* article.[201] Once again, Beale quoted from the *Official Records* in an attempt to discredit the Eleventh Corps. The Bay Stater provided the following incomplete passage taken from General Schurz's battle report:

> The Second Brigade, First Division, fell back in disorder. That brigade could only be rallied in part, and the First Brigade, First Division, was forced back also.[202]

Although Beale inferred that the general was describing the fainthearted behavior of the First Division on the evening of July 2, Schurz was actually recounting the actions of that division on the afternoon of July 1!

Undeterred by this slight of hand, Beale cited several other passages recorded by such officers as Colonel Coons of the 14th Indiana and Captain Ricketts affirming that the some of the artillery pieces on Cemetery Hill were captured and then saved by Colonel Carroll's men. Based on this testimony, Beale concluded sarcastically, that Howard's men were "'relieved' by...the 'Louisiana Tigers'...[after which]...Carroll's Brigade" arrived to save the day.

Near the end of his article, James Beale directed his discussion to the regimental monuments on East Cemetery Hill. He declared that the 106th Pennsylvania's marker appeared quite small "by reason of the pretentious monument which the 17th Conn. have reared beside it." Beale

---

out in his November 7, 1889, *National Tribune* article. "The Cannoneer" wrote: "I am satisfied that Ames's (or Harris's) Brigade did not 'break,' as I then stated, but that it simply changed front to accommodate itself to the retrograde movement of Von Gilsa's Brigade on its right, which was certainly broken, and that the 17th Connecticut, of Ames's Brigade, which held the left of the organization next to the Baltimore Pike, did not retreat at all, and was not affected by the onslaught." One must wonder how much the cries of protest from the Eleventh Corps veterans, especially A.W. Peck of the 17th Connecticut, caused Buell to change his story (Buell, *The Cannoneer*, p. 85).

[201] James Beale, "Gettysburg. The Part of the Line Occupied by Carroll's Brigade," *National Tribune*, April 2, 1891.

[202] General Schurz's remarks can be found in *O.R.*, vol. 27, part 1, p. 729.

View of the 17th Connecticut Monument

The 17th Connecticut's monument viewed from the position of the 106th Pennsylvania's marker (refer to Map 6, Appendix A for locations). James Beale compared the small marker to the Second Corps regiment to the "pretentious monument which the 17th Connecticut have *reared beside it* [author's italics]."

incorrectly implied that these monuments are very close to each other. In fact, they are separated by roughly 100 yards and only the top of the 17th's monument at the base of East Cemetery Hill is visible from the Pennsylvania regiment's marker. In a particularly inflammatory statement sure to raise the ire of many of the surviving Nutmeg veterans, Beale announced "that the relative size of the monuments is in inverse ratio to the services there rendered by the regiments erecting them."

Not surprisingly, it did not take long for General Howard's veterans to rebut Comrade Beale. Indeed, by this time the debate no longer focussed on the writings of Augustus Buell but continued unabated as different veterans began responding to each other. The May 7 issue of the *National Tribune* included a lengthy article written by W.S. Wickham, formerly of the 55th Ohio of General von Steinwehr's Second Brigade commanded by Colonel Orland Smith.[203] The Ohioan began by asserting that the "insinuations [contained in Beale's article] are so unjust to that portion of the Eleventh Corps which he [Beale] claimed was saved by the brigade [Carroll's brigade] in question." Wickham alleged that Beale was part of a group of "flippant writers ignorant of the facts...attempting to shoulder others' blunders and shortcomings onto the patient backs of the much-maligned Eleventh Corps."

Comrade Wickham was understandably incensed by Beale's comments regarding the significance of the relative sizes of the 106th Pennsylvania's and 17th Connecticut's monuments. He attempted to demonstrate the ferocity with which Harris' brigade fought on East Cemetery Hill by pointing out the much higher number of casualties suffered by this brigade relative to Colonel Carroll's command. What Wickham failed to mention, however, was that Harris' brigade suffered a good number of the casualties in the hard fighting north of Gettysburg on July 1.

At the end of his article, comrade Wickham reversed his position and admitted that Colonel Harris' brigade had been compelled to fall back because of an "impetuous charge of overwhelming numbers." Nonetheless, he qualified this statement by pointing out that other units had retreated under similar conditions. Although the old Buckeye was basically correct in his claim that Eleventh Corps men fought the

---

[203] W.S. Wickham, "Gettysburg. An Ohio Comrade Upholds the Credit of the Eleventh Corps," *National Tribune*, May 7, 1891.

Confederates hand-to-hand at the stone fence, he added that by the time Carroll's brigade arrived "the fighting was practically finished and victory won." As evidence the insistent Wickham quoted from a letter he recently had received from an unnamed officer in the 55th Ohio who had served on General Ames' staff during the battle:

> I know that Carroll's Brigade did not arrive until the attack of the enemy had been repulsed....it was almost dark, and the attack was entirely over. The Carroll Brigade [sic] had not yet arrived; and all that bombastic legend on the monument of the 14th Ind. is false. I never heard of any such claim as that contained in the clipping until I saw the Indiana monument when at Gettysburg, at the time the Ohio monuments were dedicated.[204]

Wickham's article was significant for two reasons. First, he admitted that some of the Eleventh Corps units at the base of East Cemetery Hill did fall back on the evening of July 2 but only after a hand-to-hand fight at the stone fence. Secondly, Wickham claimed that Colonel Carroll's men did not arrive until the fighting had ended thereby implying that the line was secured by rallied Eleventh Corps troops.

Two weeks after publication of Wickham's article, the *National Tribune* ran A.W. Peck's response to James Beale's most recent contribution.[205] Comrade Peck was generally correct in declaring that "Beale knows nothing about what took place at Gettysburg on the evening

---

[204] The "bombastic legend" on the 14th Indiana's monument (Appendix A) referred to by the unnamed officer is as follows: "On the evening of July 2nd 1863, a determined effort was made by Hay's and Hoke's Brigades of Early's Division of Confederate troops to carry Cemetery Hill by storm. The Union troops supporting the Batteries occupying this ground were over whelmed and forced to retire. Wiedrich's Battery was captured and two of Ricketts' guns were spiked. Carroll's Brigade, then in position south-west of the Cemetery was sent to the rescue, advancing in double quick time through the Cemetery and across the Baltimore Pike. The men went in with a cheer, the 14th Indiana met the enemy among the guns on this ground where a hand to hand struggle ensued resulting in driving the enemy from the hill."

[205] A.W. Peck, "Gettysburg," *National Tribune*, May 19, 1892.

of July 2, 1863, from personal knowledge." The former Nutmeg officer then questioned the position held by Colonel Carroll's regiments after the conclusion of the fighting on July 2 as well as the number of regiments in the brigade: "As far as I have been able to learn, there were only two [4th Ohio and 14th Indiana] regiments of Carroll's Brigade present" that evening. Continuing along the same vein, Peck recalled that the 4th Ohio "came in on our right and dropped in the grass in our rear and did nothing for there was nothing for them to do, while my regiment was heavily engaged with the enemy in our immediate front." Peck repeated Comrade Wickham's thesis that Carroll's men did not reach East Cemetery Hill until the Federal line had been secured.

Like Wickham, Peck incorrectly relied on casualty numbers to prove that General Harris' brigade "did the fighting" on the evening of July 2. Peck defiantly concluded his article by asserting that the 17th Connecticut was

> not relieved by Hayes's or Carroll's Brigades or any other troops on the evening of July 2, 1863, until after the fighting was over and the danger past, and I defy any comrade to prove to the contrary. We were there to stay, and did stay and don't you forget it![206]

A.W. Peck's piece in the *Tribune* brought a quick response from Owen Wright, formerly of the 14th Indiana.[207] Wright disdainfully noted that "Peck and his tribe say we were *not needed* [Wright's emphasis]" on the Federal right.[208] The former Hoosier infantryman correctly took Peck to task over the issue of casualties by arguing that "the Eleventh Corps'

---

[206] Peck's reference to "Hayes's" brigade is a response to James Beale's cynical comment that the Eleventh Corps troops were "relieved" by Confederate General Hays' Louisiana "Tigers."

[207] Owen Wright, "Gettysburg. Another of Carroll's Brigade Says They Held the Left of Howard's Line," *National Tribune*, June 30, 1892.

[208] Owen Wright stated that Colonel Carroll's brigade was needed on General Howard's right flank. He is mistaken here and most likely meant the right flank of Howard's line. Wright may have been referring to the Eleventh Corps left as viewed from the Confederate perspective.

loss was principally on the first day." He accounted for the generally light losses sustained by Carroll's regiments on the night of July 2 by pointing out that the men "ran down the hill to the stone wall, never halting except among the guns as before stated." Attempting to assuage offended Eleventh Corps veterans, Wright declared, "We do not impute cowardice to troops who are reinforced or helped." He defiantly summed up by claiming that Carroll's regiments "held a part of Howard's line from dark on the 2d until the 4th; and if that is a disgrace to Howard's left [sic], why it's a disgrace."

In early September 1892, Robert Collins, a former lieutenant and quartermaster of the 7th West Virginia, entered the debate by siding with Owen Wright.[209] Collins, who had not been at Gettysburg, discovered a copy of General Howard's July 29, 1863, letter to Colonel Carroll in his diary. The letter was apparently received by Carroll's headquarters on August 1, 1863 and was "published for the information of regimental and detachment commanders." Unfortunately this information did not cross General Gibbon's desk before the debate blew up in the pages of the *Army and Navy Journal* in 1864. Responding to comrade Peck's insinuation that the 7th West Virginia was not on East Cemetery Hill, Collins cited his apparently inflated recorded loss of 47 men killed and wounded in the fighting as evidence that the West Virginians were indeed in the thick of the fight.

That October one of Captain Ricketts' batterymen entered the debate because, as he put it, "both parties seem to be confident that they saved Weidrich's and Ricketts's batteries thereby preventing the defeat of the Army of the Potomac at Gettysburg."[210] Corporal William Thurston, who had been wounded in the fighting around the guns, stated that he had "no more interest in Carroll's Brigade than in Ames's." He wrote that when part of Ricketts' battery and all of Weidrich's pieces had been captured, and "it seemed as though the battle was against us, and the fate of the army hung, as it were, in the balance...Carroll's brigade...swept through the battery." Thurston inquired of comrade Peck how the Confederates got into the batteries if General Harris' brigade "stood like a stone wall and repulsed them?" Admitting that *he* cannot explain this

---

[209]Robert Collins, "At Gettysburg," *National Tribune*, September 8, 1892.

[210]W.H. Thurston, "A Ricketts Batterymen."

paradox, the artilleryman speculated that either Peck was asleep during the Confederate charge or there must have been some "arrangement with [Confederate General] Hayes [sic] and his rebels" that would explain how the "Tigers" got into the batteries. Thurston ended his article by defiantly proclaiming that "truth is truth, and the gallant charge made by Carroll's Brigade on the evening of July 2, 1863, emblazons history's brightest pages and nothing can efface it."

As expected, A.W. Peck crafted as response to Owen Wright and W.H. Thurston which was published in the November 24, 1892 issue of the *National Tribune*.[211] Responding first to Thurston's comment about his being asleep during the fighting, Peck suggested that both Thurston and Wright read the official reports, "or they may want to look up a hole to crawl into." The Nutmeg officer referred his readers to General Howard's post-battle report which Peck claimed fixed Colonel Carroll's brigade on the "extreme right of Ames's Division." Howard had actually recorded was that Carroll "moved to Ames' right." In any event, Peck, who extended his own meaning to Howard's testimony, asked the following question:

> What were Carroll's men were doing way down there near Culp's Hill [on the 'extreme right of Ames' Division'] while the fighting was going on at the top of the hill [East Cemetery Hill] for the possession of Weidrich's and Ricketts's guns?

This was a new twist on the argument; Peck believed that Carroll's men went into position just north of Culp's Hill and not on Cemetery Hill!

Comrade Peck continued this line of reasoning by pointing out that General Howard's battle report never specifically stated anything about Carroll's brigade in connection with the artillery batteries on East Cemetery Hill. While this is true and Howard did note that Captain Weidrich's battery was saved by Eleventh Corps troops, Peck assumed that these men also secured Captain Ricketts' battery. Thus he presumed that because "Carroll's Brigade is not even mentioned in connection with this struggle among the batteries...it is fair to suppose that they were not

---

[211] A.W. Peck, "At Gettysburg. Lieut. Peck Tells what Carroll's Brigade Did in the Battle," *National Tribune*, November 24, 1892.

there." Peck realized that this latest version of the fighting on East Cemetery Hill flew in the face of what W.C. Thurston had described, and simply dismissed the latter's account as the hazy recollections of a wounded man on a dark night.[212]

Peck responded to Comrade Thurston's question of how the "Tigers" got into the batteries in the first place by correctly pointing out that the Confederates exploited the gap in the line created when the 17th Connecticut was shifted to the right. Peck was also accurate in stating that rallied infantrymen of Colonel Harris' brigade, Second Division infantrymen and artillerymen, combined to save Weidrich's battery, although he incorrectly inferred that this conglomerate force saved Ricketts' guns as well. Lieutenant Peck did admit that Carroll's brigade was definitely "wanted" or needed on East Cemetery Hill, although

> instead of charging and saving the guns of Weidrich's and Ricketts's batteries, they were supporting portions of Wadsworth's Division, of the First Corps, and Ames's Division, of the Eleventh Corps, at the base of East Cemetery Hill, instead of at the top of the hill, as they pretended.

Thus Comrade Peck believed that Carroll's line, which he contended included only two regiments, stretched from the north face of Culp's Hill to the base of East Cemetery Hill!

The April 6, 1893, issue of the *National Tribune* included a response to A.W. Peck's November 1892 article.[213] William Dart, formerly of the 4th Ohio, began by dragging out General Howard's *Atlantic Monthly* article which he believed implied that the general did not request assistance and that "Carroll's Brigade was sent to him without solicitation." This was by now a dead issue. Essentially everybody, including Howard, agreed that although the former Eleventh Corps commander had forwarded a plea for relief to army headquarters, General Hancock spontaneously sent Colonel Carroll's brigade to the sounds of

---

[212] Comrade Peck failed to mention that the darkness could be used by both sides of the debate to support their respective views of the action.

[213] William T. Dart, "Carroll's Brigade. An Ohio Comrade Tells Again How They Succored the Eleventh Corps," *National Tribune*, April 6, 1893.

fighting on the right. Dart appeared to echo the same curious concern raised by John Reid eight years prior; that Carroll's brigade had been dispatched to East Cemetery Hill because of a request by Howard. Dart's argument was completely at odds with what generals Hancock and Gibbon, and almost all other Second Corps partisans, had claimed since 1864. One must wonder what Comrade Dart had been doing and reading since 1876.

William Dart castigated General Howard for not gushing enough praise for Carroll's command in his battle report. The Ohioan incorrectly claimed that the Second Corps brigade had saved both Weidrich's and Ricketts' batteries. He concluded his article by pointing out that "it is about time that comrades should cease trying to make out that no one did anything but themselves." Dart should have followed his own advice.

Comrade Dart's article closed this phase of the debate that had been initiated by publication of Augustus Buell's "The Cannoneer" series in the *National Tribune*. The final or fourth phase would not begin for another fifteen years. In the meantime, however, a number of battle histories were published. These give some clue as to which view of the fighting on East Cemetery Hill was accepted by historians of the time. In 1892 Samuel Drake published his history of the battle of Gettysburg. Writing about the threatened Union batteries on Cemetery Hill, Drake recorded that

> presently, out of the darkness, a brigade [Carroll's] of the Second Corps rushed in with a cheer. Being joined by other troops [Eleventh Corps], all fell upon the exultant Confederates, who, finding themselves left without support, saved themselves as they could.[214]

That same year First Corps historian James Henry Stine published his classic *History of the Army of the Potomac* in which he professed that General Hancock sent Carroll's brigade the Federal right "when the fighting was going on over the guns....Carroll's brigade made a charge and

---

[214]Samuel Adams Drake, *The Battle of Gettysburg 1863* (Boston: Lee and Shepard Publishers, 1892), p. 129.

drove the Confederates down the hill."[215] Two years later Henry H. Bingham synthesized much of what was known of the action on East Cemetery Hill and wrote that

> Wiedrich's Battery was captured and one or two of Ricketts' guns were spiked. At this juncture General Hancock dispatched the brave and fearless General Carroll with his gallant brigade to the scene of action. General Carroll immediately led his troops forward, attacked the enemy, and assisted by some Eleventh Corps troops quickly restored the line and recaptured the guns when the battle ended for the night.[216]

Thus in spite of the fervent debate among the veterans, most contemporary historians were able to cut through all of the rhetoric and bluster to agree that Carroll's men, in association with various Eleventh Corps regiments, arrived on East Cemetery Hill at a critical moment in the battle.

---

[215] James Henry Stine, *History of the Army of the Potomac* (Philadelphia: J.B. Rodgers Printing Company, 1892), p. 518.

[216] Henry H. Bingham, *The Second and Third Days of the Battle of Gettysburg, July 2d and 3d, 1863* (Harrisburg, Pennsylvania: E.K. Meyers, Printer, 1894), p. 14.

FINAL ARGUMENTS: 1908

Fifteen years after Williams Dart's article appeared in the pages of the *National Tribune* General Howard published his two-volume autobiography. Of the fighting on East Cemetery Hill, Howard wrote that the Louisianians "came on with a rush, broke through the front of Von Gilsa's brigade and other points of my curved front." Before he could determine where the assault was coming from, the Eleventh Corps was retreating up the east slope of the hill. The "Tigers" moved quickly into Captain Weidrich's battery. Howard ordered General Schurz to deploy reinforcements to the aid of the battling artillerymen. The former corps commander claimed that the "Tigers" were repulsed by the combined force of Schurz's reinforcements, some of Harris' rallied infantrymen and the artillerymen. General Howard also recalled that Colonel Carroll's brigade "deployed in the darkness at right angles to the general front, and swept along northward to the right...with marvelous rapidity, sweeping everything before it, till by his energetic help the entire broken front was reestablished."[217]

General Howard made no specific reference to Carroll's men in connection with any of the batteries, which no doubt distressed some of the Second Corps' veterans. Unlike twice before, however, there was no response to Howard's most recent writings. In fact, the final phase of the debate began after publication of a seemingly innocent article in the December 10, 1908, issue of the *National Tribune*.[218] The author, J.L. Dickelman, a former sergeant in the 4th Ohio, provided an imaginative, if not accurate, description of the actions of Colonel Carroll's brigade on July 2. Specifically, the Buckeye veteran implied that on the evening of July 2 the brigade moved from the Peach Orchard to the *foot* of Cemetery Hill. At that point, he continued, the brigade drove the "Tigers before us sweeping them off the crest, *thru* [Dickelman's emphasis] the Cemetery, down the hollow, over and beyond the Stone Wall, into and the thru the Wheat Field." Although Dickelman may not have meant it, he had

---

[217] Oliver Otis Howard, *Autobiography of Oliver Otis Howard* 2 volumes (New York: The Baker and Taylor Company, 1908), 1: 429.

[218] J.L. Dickelman, "Gen. Carroll's Gibraltar Brigade."

Carroll's brigade moving in a loop that started in the Peach Orchard, passed over Cemetery Hill, came through the Evergreen Cemetery and ended up near the Wheatfield.[219] The gist of Dickelman's argument, that Carroll's brigade swept the "Tigers" from the crest of Cemetery Hill, was almost lost in a bizarre description of the brigade's winding movements. This article served as a catalyst for seven more years of contention in the pages of the *National Tribune*.

The first veteran to respond to Comrade Dickelman was John Dineen, formerly of the 33rd Massachusetts.[220] Although many of Dineen's comments contained in his January 28, 1909, *National Tribune* article spoke to Dickelman's peculiar description of Colonel Carroll's movements, he did address other facets of the fighting on East Cemetery Hill. For example, the Bay State veteran seems to have questioned Dickelman's contention that the Louisiana "Tigers" breached the Federal line. More significant, however, was Dineen's claim that Carroll's brigade arrived in the rear of the 33rd! As a result, he argued, "in no way could Carroll's Brigade fire a shot, as they were in the rear of the 33d Mass. as supporters."[221] This judgment of Carroll's position sounds a bit like A.W. Peck's most recent argument that the Gibraltar Brigade arrived to the left of the Eleventh Corps line in support of General Wadsworth's First Corps troops on the north face of Culp's Hill.[222]

---

[219] Comrade Dickelman may not have been as far off the mark as it might seem. The "Wheatfield" he referred to could have been one of several that lay in the rolling terrain at the base of East Cemetery Hill (see Photographs #4 and #7 in William A. Frassanito, *Gettysburg, A Journey in Time* (New York: Charles Scribner's Sons, 1975), pp. 102-103 and 106.

[220] John Dineen, "Credit to Whom Credit is Due," *National Tribune*, January 28, 1909.

[221] Dineen appears to have ignored former Colonel Adin Underwood's description of the arrival of Colonel Carroll's brigade on East Cemetery Hill (Underwood, *Three Years Service*, pp. 130-131).

[222] Comrade Peck proposed this in his November 24, 1892, *National Tribune* article.

View of Modern Day Wainwright Avenue

View to the north along the modern Wainwright Avenue (which may be a bit farther to the left of the original brickyard lane) from a short distance north of the 33rd Massachusetts monument. Captain Ricketts' battery position is visible on the horizon at the left of the photograph. A ridge trending from left to right, down the gradient of the hill, served as a visual barrier to events taking place on Colonel Harris' front. Colonel Isaac Avery's men assaulted the Federal line deployed along a line probably a short distance to the right (east) of the roadway.

147

Dineen's article drew a quick response from A.H. Huber.[223] Although the author incorrectly claimed that the 33rd Massachusetts was "a half a mile or more" from that part of the line assaulted by the Louisiana "Tigers," the actual distance was probably well over 400 yards. According to Huber, this distance, combined with the darkness and the fact that the Massachusetts men were volleying into Hoke's Brigade, would have muddled Dineen's vision of events to the right of the North Carolinians. Thus, according to Huber, Dineen knew little of what he spoke.[224]

That April a former member of Captain Ricketts' battery weighed into the debate.[225] Oney F. Sweet had served with the crew working that "gun which was the first of Ricketts's guns reached after Wiedrick's [sic] Battery ceased firing." Although he admitted that he saw little of the fight from his position, Sweet believed that the timely appearance of Colonel Carroll's brigade kept the Confederates from gaining the second and third guns of his battery. The former batteryman was resolute in his claim that Carroll's men arrived "in the nick of time" and, with the help of shot and shell provided by Captain Greenlief Stevens' Maine battery, drove the Southerners to the base of the hill and beyond.

J.L. Dickelman's article continued to elicit responses well into the spring of 1909. S.R. Averill, also a former member of the 4th Ohio, expressed concern with Dickelman's description of the route of Colonel Carroll's charge.[226] Declaring that he did not "wish to be mean" with his former comrade, Averill maintained that Dickelman "must be off his base" in his description of what would have been a five-mile charge! Averill lamented, no doubt with tongue in cheek, that he had to wait "45 years to learn that such a charge was made at that battle." Now, even former members of Carroll's brigade were quarrelling with each other.

---

[223] A.H. Huber, "On the Right. The 33d Mass. and 'Stevens's Knoll' at Gettysburg," *National Tribune*, March 11, 1909.

[224] John Dineen's field of view would also have been obscured by a slight ridge plunging to the east from the high point of Cemetery Hill.

[225] Oney F. Sweet, "Ricketts's Battery."

[226] S.R. Averill, "The 4th Ohio at Gettysburg," *National Tribune*, May 13, 1909.

A short time later John Dineen's second article concerning the fighting on East Cemetery Hill was published in the *National Tribune*.[227] Evidently bowing to the weight of evidence, Dineen conceded that the left flank of Carroll's brigade did indeed, fire at the Confederates, although the right flank, which Dineen asserted lay in the rear of the 33rd, did not fire at all. Like just about everybody else, Dineen continued to dispute Dickelman's imagined route of attack.

Comrade Dineen had modified his opinion of the role that Colonel Carroll's men played on East Cemetery Hill and was even willing to admit that the Second Brigade "took a hand in driving back the Tigers." He qualified his admission, however, by stating that the colonel's men were simply "in the right place at the right time." Dineen expressed concern over statements made by some of Carroll's men that they "did it all." Dineen correctly asserted that the Rebels were repulsed from Ricketts' battery through a combined effort of Carroll's men and the artillerymen. He tempered this view, however, with the following passage:

> I will leave it to some of the battery boys [to] say whether the Tigers captured their guns and whether Carroll's Brigade recaptured them. As for me, I say that the Tigers got as far as the guns, and the battery boys, with the help of the infantry, beat the Tigers off or captured the most of them. Speak up, you battery boys, and defend your guns [against the claims of Carroll's men who maintain that they saved the guns?].

The *National Tribune* issue that contained John Dineen's second article also included Comrade Dickelman's second article.[228] The Buckeye wrote that he "was considerably surprised at the criticisms of Mr. Dineen [January 28, 1909] and S.R. Averill." Dickelman thanked A.H. Huber for his rejoinder to Dineen submitting that Huber "evidently likes the truth." Responding to comrade Averill's concern over the "five-mile charge," Dickelman pointed out that his previous article recounted the movements

---

[227] John Dineen, "On East Cemetery Hill," *National Tribune*, June 10, 1909.

[228] J.L. Dickelman, "Carroll's Brigade at Gettysburg," *National Tribune*, June 10, 1909.

of the brigade over much of July 2, not just the final rush to the right flank. He charged Averill with letting "his imagination loose." Dickelman then incorrectly professed that Carroll's men helped retake both Weidrich's and Ricketts' batteries. The former sergeant concluded his article by admonishing "Comrades Dineen and Averill to be sure of their facts before attempting to criticize, as imagination won't stand against facts." This advice should have been heeded by both parties to this debate.

In the end of July 1909, J.E. Murdock, formerly of the 7th West Virginia, entered the controversy.[229] The West Virginian took issue with John Dineen's understanding of the placement of various units on East Cemetery Hill on the evening of July 2. Recalling the confusion on that part of the field, Murdock wrote that "Wiedrich's Battery was overrun, his supports and his own men being swept away as with the force of a whirlwind....Howard's men had been broken and demoralized by the fierceness of the onset." It was at this decisive moment that Colonel Carroll's brigade arrived in position, quickly formed a line of battle and chased the Southerners from Ricketts' guns and back to their own lines in confusion.

The August 5 issue of the *National Tribune* contained an article written by former Captain L. Eugene C. Moore of Ricketts' battery.[230] Moore's article may have been induced by John Dineen's bid (expressed in his June 10, 1909 *National Tribune* article) to Ricketts' artillerymen to address the role that Carroll's brigade played in liberating their battery. The former officer provided a very descriptive account of the fighting on East Cemetery Hill. To supplement his own observations, Moore referred to an honest, "well-written description by 'Balch.'"[231] According the "Balch," Carroll's brigade rushed "to the rescue" of Ricketts' threatened guns, driving the Rebels before them. One wonders if this response satisfied Comrade Dineen.

---

[229] J.E. Murdock, "On Cemetery Hill."

[230] L.E.C. Moore, "Charge of the Louisianians."

[231] "Balch," otherwise known as William Balch, author of a short book on Gettysburg, was misidentified as John M. Butler in an article about Captain Ricketts and his battery published in the *Gettysburg Compiler* ("Ricketts and His Battery-The Story of an Artilleryman Who Did Some Solid Fighting," *Gettysburg Compiler*, October 12, 1886).

The October 21 issue of the *Tribune* included a lengthy article by A.F. Sweetland of the 55th Ohio.[232] Sweetland, who did not take part in the July 2 action on East Cemetery Hill, relied on Augustus Buell's book, *The Cannoneer*, for evidence that Colonel Carroll's brigade arrived on East Cemetery Hill *after* the fighting had ended. For example, the Ohioan referred to that part of the book in which Buell described Carroll's men sweeping past the artillery to the "[stone] wall, from which they routed the Rebels pell-mell."[233] Sweetland implied that by the time Carroll's three regiments arrived on East Cemetery Hill, the Rebels had been driven from the batteries to the stone fence at the bottom of the hill. The Buckeye disingenuously failed to provide the complete quotation which specifically stated that Carroll's men drove the Southerners to the stone fence and retook Weidrich's and Ricketts' guns.[234]

Continuing with his assertion that Colonel Carroll's men did not become actively engaged on East Cemetery Hill, Sweetland recounted a recent discussion he had with a Colonel C.P. Wickham of the 55th Ohio.[235] The colonel, who at the time of the battle was evidently serving on General Ames' staff, collared three German regiments which were used to help drive the Louisiana "Tigers" from Captain Weidrich's battery. Sweetland maintained that these regiments were the infantry "that Buell saw driving the Tigers from the batteries back to the stone wall a short time before he [Buell] saw Carroll's Brigade" come onto the scene. Again, this is not what Buell wrote. "The Cannoneer" maintained that he saw

---

[232] A.F. Sweetland, "Repulsing the 'Tigers' at the Cemetery," *National Tribune*, October 21, 1909.

[233] The sentence cited by Sweetland can be found in Buell, *The Cannoneer*, p. 83.

[234] The exact quotation from Augustus Buell's book (*Ibid.*) is as follows: "This [the Confederate attack] must have been very destructive to us had it continued any time, but just at that moment we heard cheers immediately on our right, and in a few seconds a splendid brigade of our infantry swept past us and charged straight at the ravine and wall, from which they routed the Rebels pell-mell, driving them clear to the bottom of the hill and retaking Weidrich's and Ricketts's guns."

[235] The colonel may have been the unnamed 55th Ohio officer who W.S. Wickham cited in his May 7, 1891, *National Tribune* article.

"some other infantry that had just come into action," the three German regiments, combine with some of Ames' men to repulse the right wing of the Confederate force. These Yankees were not the troops who moved to Ricketts' aid. Nonetheless, Sweetland concluded that his witnesses, Buell and Wickham, proved that Wiedrich's and Ricketts' batteries were saved by Eleventh Corps troops, and that "Carroll's Brigade took no part in their recapture and restoration."[236]

Undeterred by the truth, comrade Sweetland proposed that there would not have been enough time for General Hancock to receive a call for help from General Howard and for Carroll's men to reach the threatened location. However, the author conveniently forgot to mention that Hancock spontaneously dispatched Carroll's brigade to the Federal right and not in response to a summons for assistance from that sector. The Ohioan concluded his article by accusing Carroll's veterans of having been involved in a well-planned plot to "'cheat the Dutch' of their just honors."

Comrade Sweetland's lengthy article drew a quick response from Elijah Cavins, lieutenant colonel of the 14th Indiana at Gettysburg.[237] The former Hoosier officer was particularly incensed by Sweetland's claim that the 14th Indiana's and 7th West Virginia's battlefield monuments did not designate the positions where these regiments fought.[238] Pointing out that "[t]he markers of a regiment are intended to be at the advance lines of the regiment in battle," Cavins provided a detailed discussion of the fighting on the evening of July 2 designed to convince the reader that the monuments were correctly placed.

The September 1, 1910, issue of the *National Tribune* included a rambling letter by Jonah Bayles, formerly of the 7th West Virginia.[239] Bayles, replying to A.F. Sweetland, claimed to have never seen troops other than "artillerymen, the Johnnies and Carroll's Brigade" on East

---

[236] Refer to Buell, *The Cannoneer*, p. 83, for the mentioned quotations.

[237] E.H.C. Caines, "A Gettysburg Diary."

[238] Sweetland appears to have been referring to the 7th West Virginia's and 14th Indiana's markers along the modern Wainwright Avenue, and not the larger monuments near the top of the hill.

[239] Jonah Bayles, "On Cemetery Hill," *National Tribune*, September 1, 1910.

Cemetery Hill. He evidently believed that there were no Eleventh Corps men involved in the fighting on East Cemetery Hill! Clearly, Bayles was as incorrect as those veterans who claimed that Carroll's brigade arrived on East Cemetery Hill after the fighting had ended. The longer the debate went on, the stranger the stories became.

In the early part of the twentieth century, as the surviving veterans quarrelled in the pages of the *National Tribune*, several histories of the battle of Gettysburg were published. Robert Beecham's ***Gettysburg-The Pivotal Battle of the Civil War*** was printed in 1911. Writing about the fighting on East Cemetery Hill, Beecham declared that the assault on the Eleventh Corps line at the base of the hill was so sudden that General Howard's regiments "soon gave way before the rush of the fiery Tigers." The Southerners got into Ricketts' battery, captured two of the pieces and fought the artillerymen hand-to-hand for the other guns. "A moment later," Beecham continued, "the infantry line was reinforced by Carroll's brigade of Hancock's division...which dashed down the slope of Cemetery Hill, clearing both lane and ravine."[240] Two years later, ***The Battle of Gettysburg***, written by Jesse Bowman Young, formerly of the 84th Pennsylvania, was published. Young wrote that Carroll's three regiments "came at the double quick, and in spite of the darkness found positions where they could lend instant aid."[241] In 1915, the *National Tribune* published former *Toledo Blade* editor John McElroy's series of articles on the battle of Gettysburg. Writing of the fighting on East Cemetery Hill, McElroy affirmed that Colonel von Gilsa's brigade along the stone fence,

> which had been shattered by the fighting of the first day...was quickly overpowered and driven [by Hoke's Brigade]. The same fate befell Ames's Brigade, and this uncovered Rickett's [sic] and Weidrick's [sic] batteries.

Crediting General Hancock for "keeping his finger on every pulse of the battle," McElroy stated that "Carroll's well-tried brigade [moved] to the

---

[240] Robert K. Beecham, ***Gettysburg. The Pivotal Battle of the Civil War*** (Chicago, Illinois: A.C. McClurg & Co., 1911), pp. 199-200.

[241] Jesse Bowman Young, ***The Battle of Gettysburg*** (New York: Harper & Brothers Publishers, 1913, p. 274.

rescue of the batteries [along with] some other troops of Schurz's Division."[242] McElroy's version, which was fair and did not slight any particular command at the expense of another, appears to have become the prevailing view of the fight for East Cemetery Hill.

As World War I loomed on the horizon and the number of veterans of the fighting on East Cemetery Hill dwindled, so did the the ardor with which Colonel Carroll's and General Howard's partisans debated each other. Probably the last shot fired in the pages of the *National Tribune* was an article written by Hoosier Charles Myerhoff.[243] Comrade Myerhoff, whose first article detailed the action on the east slope of Cemetery Hill was published 40 years earlier, recounted his observations of the fighting. He referred to the writings of Augustus Buell and artilleryman William Thurston to argue that

> Carroll's Brigade, which, like a rushing torrent, swept thru the battery [Ricketts'], and the famous Louisiana Tigers, who played so much havoc on that fateful night, went out in darkness to molest no more that night.

Myerhoff then assailed A.W. Peck of the 17th Connecticut for statements the latter had made in a *National Tribune* article published 23 years earlier in 1892! The Hoosier pondered how the Confederates got into the artillery batteries if, as Peck had inferred, "Ames's Brigade stood like a stone wall." As further evidence of the important role played by Carroll's brigade on East Cemetery Hill, Myeroff quoted former Colonel Andrew L. Harris, commander of General Ames' brigade on the evening of July 2. At a reunion of the 4th Ohio more than 40 years after the battle, Harris, then Governor of Ohio, recalled that a part of his brigade

> was forced back until the batteries were uncovered and taken by the enemy. At this crucial point the 4th Ohio, 7th West Virginia and 14th Ind. of Carroll's Brigade,

---

[242] John McElroy, "The Battle of Gettysburg. The Story of the Action of the Different Regiments Defending Little Round Top is Continued," *National Tribune*, August 12, 1915.

[243] Charles H. Myerhoff, "Carroll's Brigade. Its Famous 20-Minutes' Work at Gettysburg," *National Tribune*, October 14, 1915.

Second Corps, came to the rescue, charged the enemy and triumphantly recaptured the batteries and repulsed the attack.[244]

---

[244] Quoted in *Ibid*.

EPILOGUE

The debate between the Second and Eleventh Corps veterans had essentially ended by 1910. Many of the participants were gone and most Americans were preoccupied with other things. The majority of battle histories written near the turn of the century, espoused the view that Colonel Carroll's brigade had indeed arrived at the scene of the fighting on East Cemetery Hill just in time to help drive the Rebels out of Captain Ricketts' battery. Nevertheless, some opposing views of the events of the evening of July 2 materialized in print. For example, James Stuart Montgomery's *The Shaping of a Battle: Gettysburg* published in 1959, just before the Civil War Centennial, espoused the early account of this action that held that Carroll's brigade had been dispatched toward the Federal right in response to General Howard's urgent request for help.[245] As described earlier, Howard, for whatever reasons, had changed his opinion of the conditions under which the Gibraltar Brigade was sent to East Cemetery Hill. Unfortunately, except for his post-battle report, Colonel Carroll never weighed in with his impressions of the circumstances surrounding the appearance of his brigade on the Army's of the Potomac's right flank.

In what most people agree to be the most exhaustive single study of the Gettysburg campaign and battle, Edwin Coddington wrote that General Hancock, who had foreseen Howard's need for reinforcements, sent Carroll's brigade toward the sounds of fighting. The three Second Corps regiments, along with "the stiffening of the Eleventh Corps resistance," repulsed the Confederates from the batteries on the hill.[246] The author of a recently published book detailing the actions of the various Connecticut regiments and batteries at Gettysburg, however, subscribed to a view of events on East Cemetery Hill more in line with what Eleventh Corps veterans A.W. Peck, A.F. Sweetland and W.S. Wickham had championed. Charles P. Hamblin wrote that

---

[245] James Stuart Montgomery, *The Shaping of a Battle: Gettysburg* (Philadelphia: Chilton Book Company, 1959), pp. 118-119.

[246] Coddington, *Gettysburg Campaign*, pp. 427, 437-438.

although Howard's troops had by now contained and driven back the Rebel assault, Col. Samuel S. Carroll, the fiery leader of this fresh brigade, insisted on getting into the action.

Hamblin asserted that Carroll sent his men down the east slope of Cemetery Hill where they "managed to strike the rear of the Southern retreating columns and capture some prisoners."[247]

In his recent analysis of the fighting on East Cemetery Hill, Harry Pfanz appears to have used General Howard's initial explanation (contained in the general's after-battle report) of the conditions under which Colonel Carroll's brigade was dispatched to thr right. Pfanz wrote that Howard "sent for help. General Hancock responded at once by suggesting to General Gibbon" that Carroll's unit should be sent to the right. The author seems to imply that Hancock responded to Howard's summons for help, a view that would not have set well with most Second Corps veterans and partisans.[248] Thus the debate continues to this day.

Colonel Carroll's men were involved in a short but spirited action on the evening of July 2, 1863 on East Cemetery Hill. Their part of the fighting, which one man recalled lasted no more than a few moments, meant much to these veterans of other fields. For the next 50 years, they would battle hard trying to prove they had played a pivotal role in securing the imperiled Federal right flank on that evening. Similarly, Eleventh Corps veterans devoted an equal amount of time and energy striving to demonstrate that they too had fought valiantly on East Cemetery Hill against overwhelming numbers. Even after being forced back, these denigrated troops had rallied around their artillery and, with other Eleventh Corps regiments rushed to the menaced part of the field, helped repulse the Southerners. General Howard's men felt especially compelled to protect their honor in light of their allegedly poor behavior at Chancellorsville and in the fighting north of Gettysburg on July 1. Many of these men were also the focus of base anti-German sentiment among the officer corps of the Army of the Potomac.

---

[247] Charles P. Hamblin (Walter L. Powell, editor), *Connecticut Yankees at Gettysburg* (Kent, Ohio: The Kent State University Press, 1993), pp. 63-64.

[248] Pfanz, *Culp's Hill and Cemetery Hill*, p. 263; Pfanz admitted that both Howard's and Hancock's versions could have been correct.

Who was right? Both parties endeavored to portray their respective roles in the best light; to this end, both sides engaged in a certain amount of truth bending, if not outright lying. Clearly, the tenuous Confederate hold on East Cemetery Hill would have failed for lack of sufficient reserves. Nonetheless, the wavering Louisianians and Tarheels were ultimately driven back from the batteries by the combined efforts of Second and Eleventh Corps troops ordered to the threatened area, General Ames' rallied units and Weidrich's and Ricketts' batterymen. The quarrel, which appears to have been rooted in a simple misunderstanding between Second and Eleventh Corps officers less than seven months after the battle, unfolded into several distinct periods of feuding. As the years passed and memories faded, the debate escalated. Perhaps the words of a former member of Captain Ricketts' battery best explain the reason for this prolonged controversy among honorable men who had, in the past, fought for basically the same reasons:

> When there are so many 'lightning charges' at a time like that, a half dozen descriptions may be given, all different, and yet all may be right. What may have been 30 minutes actual time seemed like five minutes to one man, a whole hour to another. So that 46 years afterward, to make positive assertions as to time, places, distances, and names seems unreasonable.[249]

---

[249] L.E.C. Moore, "Charge of the Louisianians."

APPENDIX A

**Selected Monuments and Markers
on East Cemetery Hill**

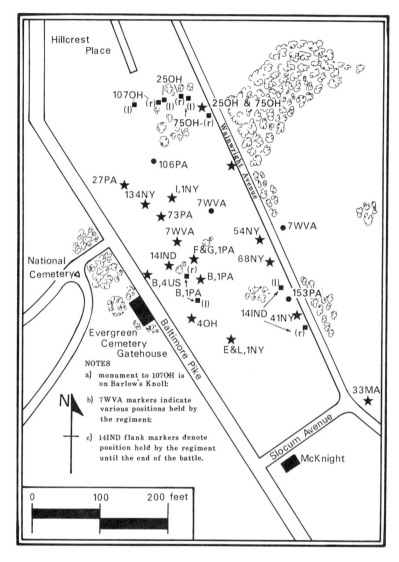

Map 6: Location of Monuments and Markers on East Cemetery Hill

Note: stars = monuments;
circles = markers;
squares = flank markers.

17th Connecticut Infantry Monument

Inscription

After a fierce contest with Early's Division at Barlow's knoll on July 1st. marked by monument there, this regiment formed in the line of battle on East Cemetery Hill and on the evening of July 2nd, took position here and was engaged in repulsing the desperate night assault of Haye's [sic] and Hokes [sic] Brigades.

dedicated: October 22, 1889.[250]

---

[250]Harrison, *Location of the Monuments*, p. 1.

14th Indiana Infantry Monument

Inscription

On the evening of July 2nd 1863, a determined effort was made by Hay's [sic] and Hoke's Brigades of Early's Division of Confederate troops to carry cemetery Hill by storm. The Union troops supporting the Batteries occupying this ground were over whelmed and forced to retire. Wiedrich's Battery was captured and two of Ricketts' guns were spiked. Carroll's Brigade, then in position south-west of the Cemetery was sent to the rescue, advancing in double quick time through the Cemetery and across the Baltimore Pike. The men went in with a cheer, the 14th Indiana met the enemy among the guns on this ground where a hand to hand struggle ensued resulting in driving the enemy from the hill. On this spot Isaac Norris, the color bearer of the 14th Ind., was killed, and many others fell nearby. The regiment then took position along the stone fence at the base of the hill south-east from this point, facing the east, the right and left flanks being designated by stone markers, there placed, which position it held to the close of the great battle.

dedicated: October 28, 1885.[251]

---

[251]*Ibid.*, p. 2.

14th Indiana Monument

14th Indiana Right Flank Marker

33rd Massachusetts Infantry Monument

Detached from the Second Brigade, Second Division, Eleventh Corps on July Second 1863. After supporting the batteries in action on Cemetery Hill, while in position in a line extending westward from near this spot, withstood and assisted in repulsing a charge of the enemy's infantry in its front.

dedicated: July 7, 1885.[252]

---

[252]*Ibid.*, p. 4.

41st New York Infantry Monument

Inscription

July 2, 3, 4, 1863.

dedicated: July 3, 1893[253]

(*New York at Gettysburg*)

---

[253]*Ibid.*, p. 8.

54th New York Infantry Monument

Inscription

July 1st skirmishing on extreme right near Rock Creek. July 2nd at sunset, severe fighting in this position. July 3rd held same position.

dedicated: July 4, 1890[254]

(New York at Gettysburg)

---

[254]*Ibid.*, p. 8.

68th New York Infantry Monument

Inscription

This regiment having participated in the first day of the battle, held this position on the 2nd and 3rd of July, 1863.

dedicated: probably sometime during 1888.[255]

(New York at Gettysburg)

---

[255]*Ibid.*, p. 8.

134th New York Infantry Monument

Inscription

July 1, 1863, this regiment was engaged about one quarter mile east of Gettysburg near York road. July 2nd and 3rd, held this position.

dedicated: July 2, 1888.[256]

(*New York at Gettysburg*)

---

[256]*Ibid.*, p. 10.

Battery I, 1st New York Light Artillery

Inscription

July 1st, 2nd, 3rd, 1863.

dedicated: May 20, 1889.[257]

(*New York at Gettysburg*)

---

[257]*Ibid.*, p. 11.

4th Ohio Infantry Monument

Inscription

On the evening of July 2, 1863, Carroll's Brigade was sent from its position with the 2nd Corps to re-enforce this position of the line, and this monument marks the position where, as part of that brigade, the 4th Ohio Infantry at that time participated in repelling an attack of the enemy.

dedicated: August 23, 1887; September 14, 1887.[258]

---

[258]*Ibid.*, p. 11.

4th Ohio Infantry Monument

Approximately 30-foot high 4th Ohio Infantry monument shortly after it was raised in 1887. Note that the upper 60% of the original monument is no longer present (compare with photograph on preceding page).

(*Ohio. **Ohio Memorials at Gettysburg. Report of the Gettysburg Memorial Commission**. Columbus, Ohio: Press of the Nitschke Brothers, 1889.*)

173

25th and 75th Ohio Infantry Monument
(this single monument commemorates both regiments on East Cemetery Hill)

Inscription

After a severe battle in the open fields beyond Gettysburg on July 1, 1863, the 11th Corps withdrew to Cemetery Hill, and at dark on July 2 this position was held by the 25th and 75th Ohio Infantry when Early's Confederate Division assaulted this hill and broke the Union line to the right, but was repulsed after a desperate hand-to-hand conflict.

dedicated: September 14, 1887.[259]

---

[259]*Ibid.*, p. 12.

25th and 75th Ohio Flank Markers

25th and 75th Ohio flank markers along remnant of the stone fence that marks their first position.

27th Pennsylvania Infantry Monument

Inscription

July 1, 1863. The regiment moved with the brigade on the afternoon to N.E. side of Gettysburg where it became actively engaged covering the retreat of the Corps. It then withdrew to this position where after dark of the 2nd it assisted in repulsing a desperate assault of the enemy. It subsequently moved into the cemetery where it remained until the close of the battle.

dedicated: September 12, 1889.[260]

(***Pennsylvania at Gettysburg***)

---

[260]*Ibid.*, p. 13.

73rd Pennsylvania Infantry Monument

Inscription

July 1st. The regiment arrived on Cemetery Hill at 2 p.m. and at a later hour moved into the town near the square to cover the retreat of the Corps. July 2nd. In the morning took position in the Cemetery. At dusk moved hastily to this position and in a severe contest assisted in repulsing a desperate assault on these batteries. July 3rd. Returned to its former position in the Cemetery and assisted in repulsing the enemy's final assault.

dedicated: September 12, 1889.[261]

(*Pennsylvania at Gettysburg*)

---

[261]*Ibid.*, p. 13.

106th Pennsylvania Infantry Marker

Inscription

'Your Batteries Can Be Withdrawn When That Regiment Runs Away' Gnl. O.O. Howard to Maj. Osborn.

dedicated: 1884-1886 (?).[262]

---
[262]*Ibid.*, p. 14.

153rd Pennsylvania Infantry Marker

Inscription

153d Regt. Penn. Vol. 1st Brigade, 1st Division 11th Corps. Engaged at Chancellorsville May 1. 2. 3. & 4. 1863. Gettysburg. July 1. 2. & 3. 1863 Erected by the Survivors

dedicated: July 1, 1884.[263]

---

[263]*Ibid.*, p. 14.

Battery B (Cooper's),
1st Pennsylvania Light Artillery Monument

Inscription

July 1, 1863: Battery arrived at 12 m. took position and was engaged between Hagerstown Road and Chambersburg Pike near Willoughby Run; changed position to the right and swept Oak Hill with its fire. Withdrew to Theological Seminary, where it fought till after 4 p.m.; retired to this position where it remained until close of heavy artillery contest with the enemy's batteries on Benner's Hill, during afternoon engagement of July 2, when relieved by Ricketts' Battery. July 3: Was engaged on left center during the final attack and second repulse of the enemy.

dedicated: September 11, 1889.[264]

---

[264]*Ibid.*, p. 16.

Battery B, 1st Pennsylvania Light Artillery Monument

(*Pennsylvania at Gettysburg*)

Batteries F and G (Ricketts'), 1st Pennsylvania Light Artillery Monument

Inscription

July 2nd. Reached the field and took this position in the afternoon and engaged the Rebel batteries on Benner's Hill. 8 p.m. A Rebel column charged the Battery and a desperate hand-to-hand conflict ensued which was repulsed after every round of canister had been fired. July 3rd. Engaged with the Rebel batteries on the left and centre of the line.

dedicated: July 4, 1894.[265]

(*Pennsylvania at Gettysburg*)

---

[265]*Ibid.*, p. 17.

7th West Virginia Infantry Monument

Inscription

A dusk July 2nd Carroll's Brigade was ordered by General Hancock to this point. "On arriving there we found the Battery about to be taken charge of by the enemy who were in large force. Whereupon we immediately charged on the enemy and succeeded in completely routing their entire force and driving them beyond our lines."

dedicated: September 28, 1898.[266]

---

[266]*Ibid.*, p. 18.

APPENDIX B

Order of Battle[267]

Units Engaged on East Cemetery Hill
Evening, July 2, 1863

---

[267] Modified from *O.R.*, vol. 27, parts 1 and 2.

ARMY OF THE POTOMAC
Major General George Gordon Meade

First Corps
Major General John F. Reynolds
Major General Abner Doubleday
Major General John Newton

Artillery Brigade
Colonel Charles S. Wainwright

Maine Light, 2nd Battery (B), *Captain James Hall*
Maine Light, 5th Battery (E), *Captain Greenleaf T. Stevens*
Lieutenant Edward N. Whittier
1st New York Light, Battery L[268], *Captain Gilbert H. Reynolds*
Lieutenant George Breck
1st Pennsylvania Light, Battery B, *Captain James H. Cooper*
4th United States, Battery B, *Lieutenant James Stewart*

Second Corps
Major General Winfield S. Hancock
Brigadier General John Gibbon
Major General Winfield S. Hancock

Second Division
Brigadier General John Gibbon
Brigadier General William Harrow
Brigadier General John Gibbon

---

[268] Battery E, 1st New York Light Artillery was attached to this battery during the battle.

Second Brigade
Brigadier General Alexander S. Webb

69th Pennsylvania Regiment
Colonel Dennis O'Kane
Captain William Davis

72nd Pennsylvania Regiment
Colonel DeWitt C. Baxter
Lieutenant Colonel Theodore Hesser

71st Pennsylvania Regiment
Colonel Richard P. Smith

106th Pennsylvania Regiment
Lieutenant Colonel William L. Curry

Third Division
Brigadier General Alexander Hays

First Brigade
Colonel Samuel S. Carroll

14th Indiana Regiment
Colonel John Coons

4th Ohio Regiment
Lieutenant Colonel Leonard W. Carpenter

8th Ohio Regiment
Lieutenant Colonel Franklin Sawyer

7th West Virginia Regiment
Lieutenant Colonel Jonathan H. Lockwood

Eleventh Corps
Major General Oliver O. Howard
Major General Carl Schurz
Major General Oliver O. Howard

First Division
Brigadier General Francis C. Barlow
Brigadier General Adelbert Ames

First Brigade
Colonel Leopold von Gilsa

41st New York Regiment
Colonel Detleo von Einsiedel

54th New York Regiment
Major Stephen Kovacs
Lieutenant Ernst

68th New York Regiment
Colonel Gotthilf Bourry

153d Pennsylvania
Major John F. Fruehauff

Second Brigade
Brigadier General Adelbert Ames
Colonel Andrew L. Harris

17th Connecticut Regiment
Lieutenant Douglas Fowler
Major Allen G. Brady

75th Ohio Regiment
Colonel Andrew L. Harris
Captain George B. Fox

25th Ohio Regiment
Lieutenant Colonel Jeremiah Williams
Captain Nathaniel J. Manning
Lieutenant William Maloney
Lieutenant Israel White

107th Ohio Regiment
Colonel Seraphim Meyer
Captain John M. Lutz

Second Division
Brigadier General Adolph von Steinwehr

First Brigade
Colonel Charles R. Coster

134th New York Regiment
Lieutenant Colonel Allan H. Jackson

154th New York Regiment
Colonel D.B. Allen

27th Pennsylvania Regiment
Lieutenant Colonel Lorenz Cantador

73rd Pennsylvania Regiment
Captain D.F. Kelley

Second Brigade
Colonel Orland Smith

33rd Massachusetts Regiment
Colonel Adin B. Underwood

55th Ohio Regiment
Colonel Charles B. Gambee

136th New York Regiment
Colonel James Wood, Jr

73rd Ohio Regiment
Lieutenant Colonel Richard Long

Third Division
Major General Carl Schurz
Brigadier General Alexander Schimmelfennig
Major General Carl Schurz

First Brigade
Brigadier General Alexander Schimmelfennig
Colonel George von Amsberg

85th Illinois Regiment
Lieutenant *Colonel Edward S. Salomon*

157th New York Regiment
Colonel Philip P. Brown, Jr.

45th New York Regiment
Colonel George von Amsberg
Lieutenant Colonel Adolphus Dobke

61st Ohio Regiment
Colonel Stephen J. McGroarty

74th Pennsylvania Regiment
Colonel Adolph von Hartung
Lieutenant Colonel Alexander von Mitzel
Captain Gustav Schleiter
Captain Henry Krauseneck

Second Brigade
Colonel Wladimir Krzyzanowski

58th New York Regiment
Lieutenant Colonel August Otto
Captain Emil Koeneg

82nd Ohio Regiment
Colonel James S. Robinson
Lieutenant Colonel David Thomson

119th New York Regiment
Colonel John T. Lockman
Lieutenant Colonel Edward F. Floyd

75th Pennsylvania Regiment
Colonel Francis Mahler
Major August Ledig

26th Wisconsin
Lieutenant Colonel Hans Boebel
Captain John W. Fuchs

Artillery Brigade
Major Thomas W. Osborn

1st New York Light, Battery I, *Captain Michael Weidrich*
New York Light, 13th Battery, *Lieutenant William Wheeler*
1st Ohio Light, Battery I, *Captain Hubert Dilger*
1st Ohio Light, Battery K, *Captain Lewis Heckman*
4th United States, Battery G,
Lieutenant Bayard Wilkeson
Lieutenant Eugene A. Bancroft

Artillery Reserve
Brigadier General Robert O. Tyler
Captain James M. Robertson

Third Volunteer Brigade

Captain James F. Huntington
New Hampshire Light, 1st Battery, *Captain Frederick M. Edgell*
1st Ohio Light, Battery H, *Lieutenant George W. Norton*
1st Pennsylvania Light, Batteries F and G, *Captain R. Bruce Ricketts*
West Virginia Light, Battery C, *Captain Wallace Hill*

ARMY OF NORTHERN VIRGINIA
General Robert E. Lee

Second Army Corps
Lieutenant General Richard S. Ewell

Early's Division
Major General Jubal A. Early

Hays' Brigade
Brigadier General Harry T. Hays

5th Louisiana Regiment
Major Alexander Hart
Captain T.H. Biscoe

7th Louisiana Regiment
Colonel D.B. Penn

6th Louisiana Regiment
Lieutenant Colonel Joseph Hanlon
Major G.A. Lester

8th Louisiana Regiment
Colonel T.D. Lewis
Lieutenant Colonel A. de Blanc

9th Louisiana Regiment
Colonel Leroy A. Stafford

Hoke's Brigade
Colonel Issac E. Avery
Colonel A.C. Godwin

6th North Carolina
Major S. McD. Tate

21st North Carolina
Colonel W.W. Kirkland

57th North Carolina Regiment
Colonel A.C. Godwin

BIBLIOGRAPHY

General Sources

Beecham, Robert K. *Gettysburg. The Pivotal Battle of the Civil War.* Chicago: A.C. McClurg & Co., 1911.

Bingham, Henry H. *The Second and Third Days of the Battle of Gettysburg, July 2d and 3d, 1863.* Harrisburg, Pennsylvania: E.K. Meyers, Printer, 1894.

Boatner, Mark M., III. *The Civil War Dictionary.* New York: David McKay Company, Inc., 1959.

Busey, John W. *These Honored Dead. The Union Casualties at Gettysburg.* Hightstown, New Jersey: Longstreet House, 1988.

Busey, John W., and Martin, David G. *Regimental Strengths and Losses at Gettysburg* Hightston, New Jersey: Longstreet House, 1986.

Christ, Elwood. *"Over a Wide, Hot,...Crimson Plain"-The Struggle for the Bliss Farm at Gettysburg.* Baltimore: Butternut and Blue, 1993.

Coddington, Edwin B. *The Gettysburg Campaign: A Study in Command.* New York: Charles Scribner's Sons, 1968.

Drake, Samuel Adams. *The Battle of Gettysburg 1863.* Boston: Lee and Shepard Publishers, 1892.

Dyer, Frederick H. *Compendium of the War of the Rebellion*, 3 volumes. New York: Thomas Yoseloff, 1959.

Felton, Silas. "Pursuing the Elusive 'Cannoneer.'" *Gettysburg Magazine 9* (July 1993): 33-39.

Frassanito, William A. *Gettysburg, A Journey in Time.* New York: Charles Scribner's Sons, 1975.

Furgurson, Ernest B. *Chancellorsville 1863. The Souls of the Brave.* New York: Alfred A. Knopf, 1992.

Hamblin, Charles P. *Connecticut Yankees at Gettysburg.* Walter L. Powell, editor, Kent, Ohio: The Kent State University Press, 1993.

Hamilton, Milton W. "Augustus C. Buell, Fraudulent Historian." *Pennsylvania Magazine of History and Biography* 80 (October 1956): 478-492.

Harrison, Kathy Georg. *The Location of the Monuments, Markers, and Tablets on Gettysburg Battlefield.* Gettysburg, Pennsylvania: Thomas Publications, 1993.

Krick, Robert K. *Lee's Colonels.* 4th Edition. Dayton, Ohio: Press of the Morningside Bookshop, 1992.

Lang, T.F. *Loyal West Virginia from 1861 to 1865.* Baltimore, Maryland: The Deutsch Publishing Co., 1895.

Lonn, Ella. *Foreigners in the Union Army and Navy.* Baton Rouge, Louisiana: Louisiana State University Press, 1951.

Miller, Francis Trevelyan, ed. *The Photographic History of the Civil War in Ten Volumes*, 10 Volumes. New York: The Review of Reviews, Co., 1911.

Montgomery, James Stuart *The Shaping of a Battle: Gettysburg.* Philadelphia: Chilton Book Company, 1959.

New York Monuments Commission for the Battlefields of Gettysburg and Chattanooga, *Final Report on the Battlefield of Gettysburg*, 3 volumes, William F. Fox, editor, Albany, New York: J.B. Lyon Company, Printers, 1902.

Ohio. *Ohio Memorials at Gettysburg. Report of the Gettysburg Memorial Commission.* Columbus, Ohio: Press of the Nitschke Brothers, 1889.

Paris, Louis Philippe Albert d'Orleans, Comte de. *History of the Civil War in America.* 4 volumes. Translated by Louis F. Tasistro. Volumes 1 and 2 edited by Henry Coppee. Volumes 3 and 4 edited by John P. Nicholson. Philadelphia: Porter & Coates, 1875-1888.

Pennsylvania. Gettysburg Battlefield Commission. *Pennsylvania at Gettysburg. Ceremonies at the Dedication of the Monuments Erected by the Commonwealth of Pennsylvania to Mark the Positions of the Pennsylvania Commands Engaged in the Battle.* 2 volumes. John P. Nicholson, editor, Harrisburg, Pennsylvania: W.S. Ryan, State Printers, 1904.

Pfanz, Harry W. *Gettysburg-The Second Day.* Chapel Hill, North Carolina: The University of North Carolina Press, 1987.

Pfanz, Harry W. *Gettysburg-Culp's Hill and Cemetery Hill.* Chapel Hill, North Carolina: The University of North Carolina Press, 1993.

Priest, John M. *Antietam: The Soldiers' Battle.* Shippensburg, Pennsylvania: White Mane Publishing, Co., Inc., 1989.

Raus, Edmund J., Jr. *A Generation on the March-The Union Army at Gettysburg*. Lynchburg, Virginia: H.E. Howard, Inc., 1987.

Reid, Whitelaw. *Ohio in the War; Her Statesmen, Her Generals, and Soldiers*, 2 volumes, Cincinnati, Ohio; Moore, Wilstach and Baldwin, 1868.

Sauers, Richard A. *The Gettysburg Campaign, June 3-August 1*. Westport, Connecticut: Greenwood Press, 1982.

Scott, Robert Garth. *Into the Wilderness with the Army of the Potomac*. 2nd Edition, Revised. Bloomington, Indiana; Indiana University Press, 1992.

Sifakis, Stewart. *Who Was Who in the Civil War*. New York; Facts On File, Inc., 1988.

United States War Department. *The War of the Rebellion: A Compilation of the Official Records of the Union and Confederate Armies*. 128 volumes, Washington, D.C.: U.S. Government Printing Office, 1880-1901.

Warner, Ezra J. *Generals in Blue*. Baton Rouge, Louisiana; Louisiana State University Press, 1964.

Young, Jesse Bowman. *The Battle of Gettysburg*. New York: Harper & Brothers Publishers, 1913.

Unit Histories

Baxter, Nancy Niblick. *Gallant Fourteenth. The Story of an Indiana Civil War Regiment*. Traverse City, Indiana: Pioneer Study Center Press, 1980.

Clark, Walter (compiler), *Histories of the Several Regiments and Battalions from North Carolina in the Great War 1861-65*, 5 volumes. Raleigh and Goldsboro, North Carolina; State of North Carolina, 1901.

Culp, Edward C. *The Twenty-Fifth Ohio Veteran Volunteer Infantry in the War for the Union*. Topeka, Kansas: George W. Crane & Company, Printers, 1885.

Keifer, W.R. *History of the One Hundred and Fifty-third Regiment Pennsylvania Volunteers*. Easton, Pennsylvania: Press of the Chemical Publishing Co., 1909.

Kepler, William. *History of the Three Months and Three Years' Service of the Fourth Regiment Ohio Volunteer Infantry in the War for the Union.* Cleveland, Ohio; Leader Printing Co., 1886.

Martin, David G. *Carl Bornemann's Regiment. The Forty-First New York Infantry.* Hightstown, New Jersey: Longstreet House, 1987.

Remington, Cyrus Kingsbury. *A Record of Battery I, First N.Y. Light Artillery Vols. Otherwise Known as Wiedrich's Battery During the War of the Rebellion, 1861-'65.* Buffalo, New York: Press of the Courier Company, 1891.

Sawyer, Franklin. *A Military History of the 8th Regiment Ohio Volunteer Infantry, Its Battles, Marches and Army Movements.* Cleveland, Ohio; Fairbanks, 1881.

Sawyer, Franklin. *The Eighth Ohio at Gettysburg. Address by General Franklin Sawyer.* Washington, D.C.: Regimental Association, E.J. Gray, Printer, 1889.

Stine, James Henry. *History of the Army of the Potomac.* Philadelphia: J.B. Rodgers Printing Company, 1892.

Underwood, Adin B. *The Three Years Service of the Thirty-Third Massachusetts Infantry, 1862-1865.* Boston: A. Williams & Company, Publishers, 1881.

Walker, Francis A. *History of the Second Army Corps in the Army of the Potomac.* New York; Charles Scribner's Sons, 1887.

Ward, Joseph R.C. *History of the One Hundred and Sixth Regiment, Pennsylvania Volunteers.* Philadelphia: Grant, Fiares & Rodgers, 1883.

Published Diaries and Personal Narratives

Adjutant (pseud.). "Congress and General Howard." *Army and Navy Journal*, March 12, 1864.

Agassiz, George R. (editor). *Meade's Headquarters, 1863-1865, Letters of Colonel Theodore Lyman, From the Wilderness to Appomattox.* Boston, Massachusetts: Massachusetts Historical Society, 1922.

Averill, S.R. "The 4th Ohio at Gettysburg" *National Tribune*, May 13, 1909.

Bayles, Jonah. "On Cemetery Hill." *National Tribune*, September 1, 1910.

Beale, James. "Gettysburg, A Review of Gen. Howard's Account of the Battle." *National Tribune*, January 1, 1885.

Beale, James. "Gettysburg. Some Facts for the Eleventh Corps to Digest." *National Tribune*, March 13, 1890.

Beale, James. "Gettysburg. The Part of the Line Occupied by Carroll's Brigade." *National Tribune*, April 2, 1891.

Buell, Augustus. "Story of a Cannoneer. Battle of Gettysburg." *National Tribune*, November 7, 1889.

Buell, Augustus. "Story of a Cannoneer. The Eleventh Corps at Chancellorsville and Gettysburg." *National Tribune*, November 28, 1889.

Buell, Augustus. "Note." *National Tribune*, December 26, 1889.

Buell, Augustus. *The Cannoneer. Recollections of Service in the Army of the Potomac*. Washington, D.C.: The National Tribune, 1890.

Caines [Cavins], E.H.C. "A Gettysburg Diary, Carroll's Brigade and the Part It Played in Repulsing the Tigers." *National Tribune*, December 23. 1909.

Carroll's Brigade (pseud.). "Gen. Howard and Gettysburg." *Chicago Tribune*, July 2, 1876.

Collins, Robert. "At Gettysburg." *National Tribune*, September 8, 1892.

Dart, William T. "Carroll's Brigade. An Ohio Comrade Tells Again How They Succored the Eleventh Corps." *National Tribune*, April 6, 1893.

Dickelman, J.L. "Gen. Carroll's Gibraltar Brigade at Gettysburg, Fighting on Different Parts of the Line." *National Tribune*, December 10, 1908.

Dickelman, J.L. "Carroll's Brigade at Gettysburg." *National Tribune*, June 10, 1909.

Dineen, John. "Credit to Whom Credit is Due." *National Tribune*, January 28, 1909.

Dineen, John. "On East Cemetery Hill." *National Tribune*, June 10, 1909.

F (pseud.). "Gettysburg. A Spirited Account of the Battle, and the Part Taken Therein by the 8th Ohio." *National Tribune*, August 20, 1885.

Fischer, Louis. *National Tribune*, April 3, 1890.

Fiske, Samuel W. (editor). *Mr. Dunn Browne's Experiences in the Army*. New York: Nichols and Noyes, 1866.

"14th Indiana," *Rockwell Tribune*, September 12, 1889.

Galwey, Thomas F. *The Valiant Hours*. Harrisburg, Pennsylvania: The Stackpole Company, 1961.

Gibbon, John. *Personal Recollections of the Civil War*. New York: G.P. Putnam's Sons, 1928; reprint edition, Dayton, Ohio: Press of the Morningside Bookshop, 1978.

Houghton, William. "Carroll's Brigade at Gettysburg." *National Tribune*, November 28, 1889.

Howard, Oliver O. *Washington Daily Chronicle*, March 27, 1864.

Howard, Oliver O., "Campaign and Battle of Gettysburg," *Atlantic Monthly* 38 (July 8, 1876): 48-71.

Howard, Oliver O. "Personal Reminiscences of the War of the Rebellion; XLVII." *National Tribune*, January 1, 1885.

Howard, Oliver O. *Autobiography of Oliver Otis Howard*, 2 volumes. New York: The Baker and Taylor Company, 1908.

Huber, A.H. "On the Right. The 33d Mass. and 'Stevens's Knoll' at Gettysburg." *National Tribune*, March 11, 1909.

Hunt, Henry J. "The Second Day at Gettysburg." *The Century Magazine* 23 (December 1886): 278-95.

Ladd, David L., and Ladd, Audrey J. (editors). *The Bachelder Papers. Gettysburg in Their Own Words*, 3 volumes. Dayton, Ohio: Press of the Morningside Bookshop, 1994, 1995.

M (pseud.). "Gettysburg. What the 14th Ind. Did in the Fight." *National Tribune*, September 10, 1885.

McClure, J.R. "Old Bricktop." *National Tribune*, December 5, 1889.

McElroy, John. "The Battle of Gettysburg. The Story of the Action of the Different Regiments Defending Little Round Top is Continued." *National Tribune*, August 12, 1915.

Moore, L.E.C. "Charge of the Louisianians." *National Tribune*, August 5, 1909.

Murdock, J.E. "On Cemetery Hill." *National Tribune*, July 29, 1909.

Myerhoff, Charles H. "What Troops did Carroll's Brigade Displace in the Charge." *National Tribune*, April 24, 1890.

Myerhoff, Charles H. "At Gettysburg." *National Tribune*, April 24, 1890.

Myerhoff, Charles H. "Carroll's Brigade. Its Famous 20-Minutes' Work at Gettysburg." *National Tribune*, October 14, 1915.

Nevins, Allan (editor). *A Diary of Battle: The Personal Journals of Colonel Charles S. Wainwright, 1861-1865*. New York:

Harcourt, Brace & World, 1962; reprint edition, Gettysburg: Stan Clark Military Books, 1993.

One Who Knows (pseud.). "Congress and General Howard." *Army and Navy Journal*, March 19, 1864.

Osborn, Thomas W. "The Artillery at Gettysburg." *Philadelphia Weekly Times*, May 31, 1879.

Peck, A.W. "Gettysburg. The Part Taken by the Eleventh Corps." *National Tribune*, December 12, 1889.

Peck, A.W. *National Tribune*, April 10, 1890.

Peck, A.W. "Gettysburg." *National Tribune*, May 19, 1892.

Peck, A.W. "At Gettysburg. Lieut. Peck Tells what Carroll's Brigade Did in the Battle." *National Tribune*, November 24, 1892.

Reid, John G. "Gettysburg." *National Tribune*, January 22, 1885.

"Ricketts and His Battery-The Story of an Artilleryman Who Did Some Solid Fighting." *Gettysburg Compiler*, October 12, 1886.

Scott, Robert Garth (editor). *Fallen Leaves. The Civil War Letters of Major Henry Livermore Abbott*. Kent, Ohio: The Kent State University Press, 1991.

Schurz, Carl. *The Reminiscences of Carl Schurz*, 3 volumes. New York: McClure Company, 1907-08.

Second Corps (pseud.). "Gen. Howard and Gettysburg." *Chicago Tribune*, June 30, 1876.

Silverman, Jason H. (editor). "'The Excitement Had Begun!' The Civil War Diary of Lemuel Jefferies, 1862-1863." *Manuscripts* 30 (Fall 1978): 265-78.

Sweet, Oney F. "Ricketts's Battery." *National Tribune*, April 29, 1909.

Sweetland, A.F. "Repulsing the 'Tigers' at the Cemetery." *National Tribune*, October 21, 1909.

The Congressional Globe. The Official Proceedings of Congress. 38th Congress, 1st Session, 1864.

Thurston, W.H. "A Ricketts Batterymen Supports Carroll's Brigade Claim." *National Tribune*, October 3, 1892.

Truth (pseud.). "Congress and General Howard." *Army and Navy Journal*, February 10, 1864.

Truth (pseud.) "Congress and General Howard." *Army and Navy Journal*, April 2, 1864.

Wickham, W.S. "Gettysburg. An Ohio Comrade Upholds the Credit of the Eleventh Corps." *National Tribune*, May 7, 1891.

Wright, Owen. "Gettysburg. Another of Carroll's Brigade Says They Held the Left of Howard's Line." *National Tribune*, June 30, 1892.

Unpublished Letters and Papers

David E. Beem. Gettysburg Speech, 1887. United States Army Military History Institute, Carlisle Barracks, Carlisle, Pennsylvania.

David Beem. "History of the Fourteenth Indiana Volunteers." Beem Papers. Indiana Historical Society Library, Indianapolis, Indiana.

David H. Beem. Letter to Wife. July 5, 1863. United States Army Military History Institute, Carlisle Barracks, Carlisle, Pennsylvania.

Charles B. Brockway to David McConaughy. March 5, 1864. Peter F. Rothermel Papers. Pennsylvania State Archives, Harrisburg, Pennsylvania.

200

INDEX

A

"Adjutant" 103, 103(n. 148), 104
Alexandria, Virginia 7
Ames, Brigadier General Adelbert 56, **57**, 93, 109, 112, 118, 137
Amsberg, Colonel George von 124
Andrews, Lieutenant Colonel Richard Snowden 50(n. 75)
Antietam, Battle of 11
Army and Navy Journal 100, 103, 103(n. 148), 104, 105, 106, 139
Atlantic Monthly 110, 111, 112, 114, 141
Averill, S.R. **(4th Ohio Infantry)** 148, 149
Avery, Colonel Isaac 52, **55**, 72

B

Bachelder, John B. 32-33(n. 47), 109
"Balch" (William Balch) 150, 150(n. 231)
Ball's Bluff, Virginia 20
Baltimore and Ohio Railroad 5
Baltimore Pike 32, 63, 63(n. 82), 72, 82, 83, **86**, 87, 89, 116
Barlow, Brigadier General Francis C. 52, 56, 116, 131
Barnesville, Maryland 22
Bayles, Jonah **(7th West Virginia Infantry)** 152
Beale, James **(12th Massachusetts Infantry)** 112, 126-127, 129, 130, 131, 134, 135, 136, 137
Beecham, Robert 153
Beem, David **(14th Indiana Infantry)** 42, 82, 83, 88(n. 114)
Benner's Hill, Gettysburg, Pennsylvania 50
Beverely, West Virginia 5
Bingham, Henry H. 143
Birney, Major General David B. 108
Bliss Farm, Gettysburg, Pennsylvania 35
Brandy Station, Virginia 18
Breck, Lieutenant George **(Batteries E and L, 1st New York Light Artillery)** 63
Brian Farm, Gettysburg, Pennsylvania 32
Brian Tenant Buildings, Gettysburg, Pennsylvania 37, 41
Brady, Major Allen G. **(17th Connecticut Infantry)** 69, **70**, 71, 93(n. 127)

Brockway, Lieutenant Charles **(Batteries F and G, 1st Pennsylvania Light Artillery)** 69, 79(n. 103), 80, **81**
Browne, Dunn **(14th Connecticut Infantry)** 125(n. 180)
Browne, Captain N. 76-77(n. 97)
Buell, Augustus ("The Cannoneer") **(Battery B, 4th United States Artillery)** 120, 120(n. 174), **121**, 122, 124, 124(n. 178), 125, 126, 130, 131, 133, 133-134(n. 200), 136, 142, 151-152, 151(n. 234), 154
Burnside, Major General Ambrose E. 12
Buschbeck, Colonel Adolphus 129
Butterfield, Major General Daniel, Chief of Staff, Army of the Potomac 23(n. 33)
Butler, John M. 150(n. 231)

C

Camp Dennison, Ohio 3, 5
Camp Jackson, Ohio 3
Cameron, West Virginia 5
Cantador, Lieutenant Colonel Lorenz **(27th Pennsylvania Infantry)** 124
Carroll, Colonel Samuel Sprigg 1, 3, 7, 12, **14**, 15, 15(n. 19), 16, 19, 22, 28, 32, 32-33(n. 47), 35, 37, 39, 43, 45, 46, 47, 47(n. 70), 49, 82, 83, 93, 98, 100, 102, 103, 104, 105, 107, 109, 113, 114, 116, 125, 125(n. 180), 126, 143, 148, 156, 157
Carpenter, Lieutenant Colonel Leonard W. **(4th Ohio Infantry)** 43, **44**
Cavins, Lieutenant Colonel Elijah H.C. **(14th Indiana Infantry)** 25, 25(n. 38), **26**, 42, 94(n. 134), 152
Cemetery Hill, Gettysburg, Pennsylvania 32(n. 45), 45(n. 65), 46, 50, 63, 77, 82, 93, 104, 110(n. 158), 134, 140, 144, 145, 157
Cemetery Ridge, Gettysburg, Pennsylvania 28, 32, 32-33(n. 47), 35, 37, 41, 42, 45
Centreville, Virginia 18
Century Magazine, The 132
Chancellorsville, Battle of 1, 12, 56, 99, 116, 122, 129, 131, 157
Cheat Mountain, West Virginia 3, 5
Chicago Tribune 111
Civil War Centennial 156
Coddington, Edwin B. 1-2, 156
Collins, Robert **(7th West Virginia Infantry)** 139
Confederate Forces
    Army of Northern Virginia 7, 12, 16, 20
    Confederate Corps
        Ewell's Corps 51
        A.P. Hill's Corps 108

Longstreet's Corps 108
Confederate Divisions
Johnson's Division 52
Confederate Brigades
G.B. Anderson's Brigade 8
Davis' Brigade 108
Gordon's Brigade 8
Henagan's Brigade 108
Hoke's (Avery's) Brigade 52, **64**, **65**, 66, **68**, 71, 72, **73**, 92, **146**, **147**, 148, 153
Louisiana Tigers (H.T. Hays' Brigade) **59**, 61, 63, 71, 72, 76, 77, 89, 91, 111, 112, 113, 118, 134, 140, 141, 144, 145, 148, 149, 153, 154
Posey's Brigade 43
Wright's Brigade 43
Confederate Regiments
5th Louisiana Infantry Regiment 52
6th Louisiana Infantry Regiment 52
7th Louisiana Infantry Regiment 52
8th Louisiana Infantry Regiment 52, 74
9th Louisiana Infantry Regiment 52, 79(n. 101)
6th North Carolina Infantry Regiment 52, 79(n. 101)
21st North Carolina Infantry Regiment 52, 69
57th North Carolina Infantry Regiment 52
Confederate Battalions/Batteries
Latimer's Artillery Battalion 50
Lee Battery 50
Congress, 38th 99
Congressional Resolution of Thanks 99, 99(n. 142), 100, 102
Coons, Colonel John **(14th Indiana Infantry)** 22, 32-33(n. 47), 35, **36**, 83, 87, 87(n. 115), 89(n. 120), 91, 134
Coster, Colonel Charles R. 124
Couch, Major General Darius N. 12
Culp, Edward C. **(25th Ohio Infantry)** 118, 119
Culp's Hill, Gettysburg, Pennsylvania 46(n. 69), 48, 50, 52, 63, **73**, 110(n. 158), 131(n. 193), 132, 140, 141, 145
Culpeper Court House, Virginia 16, 93
Custer, Brigadier General George A. 15

D

Daily Chronicle, Washington 106-107

Dart, William **(4th Ohio Infantry)** 141, 142, 144
Davis, Brigadier General Joseph R. 108
Dickelman, J.L. **(4th Ohio Infantry)** 45(n. 65), 92-93, 144-145, 145(n. 219), 148, 149-150
Dineen, John **(33rd Massachusetts Infantry)** 145, 145(n. 221), 148, 149, 150
Drake, Samuel 142

E

Early, Major General Jubal A. 50, **53**, 91, 104
East Cemetery Hill, Gettysburg, Pennsylvania 1, 46(n. 69), 47, 47(n. 70), 50, 56, 61, 63, 63(n. 82), **64**, **65**, 66, 74, 76-77(n. 97), 83(n. 111), 87(n. 115), **88**, 91, 92, 93, 94, 95, 96, 98, 102, 104, 105, 107, 108, 109, 110, 111, 111(n. 160), 112, 113, 114, 116, 118, 119, 120, 126, 131, 132, 133, 134, 136, 137, 138, 139, 140, 141, 142, 143, 145, 145(n. 219), 145(n. 221), 149, 150, 151, 153, 154, 157, 158
Edinburg, Virginia 7
Emmitsburg Road 35, 37, 39, 41, 45, 47, 50
Evergreen Cemetery, Gettysburg, Pennsylvania 47, 63, 74(n. 93), 144, 145
Evergreen Cemetery Gate 63, **68**, 83, **85**, **86**
Ewell, Lieutenant General Richard S. 50, 50(n. 76), **51**, 52

F

"F" **(8th Ohio Infantry)** 114
Falmouth, Virginia 12
Folly Island, South Carolina 99
Fort Gaines 8(n. 13)
Fort Sumter 3
Frederick, Maryland 24
Fredericksburg, Battle of 12, 15
Fredericksburg, Virginia 2, 7, 11
French, Major General William H. 7-8, **9**, 12, 19
Front Royal, Virginia 7

G

Gainesville, Virginia 19
Galwey, Lieutenant Thomas Francis **(8th Ohio Infantry)** 20, 22, 23, 23(n. 33), 27-28, 33, 32-33(n. 47), 39

General Orders 67 25, 27
Germans (anti-German sentiment) 56, 116-117, 116-117(n. 168), 117(n. 169), 122, 124, 124(n. 178), 126, 151, 157
Gettysburg, Battle (and Campaign) of 1, 2, 95, 98, 99, 100, 102, 109, 120, 124, 131, 137, 139, 142, 153, 156
Gettysburg, Pennsylvania 1, 15, 24, 25, 27, 28, 32, 61, 63, 136, 157
Gettysburg Compiler 150(n. 231)
Gibbon, Brigadier General John 46, 46(n. 67), 46(n. 69), 100, **101**, 102, 103(n. 145), 103, 103(n. 148), 104, 105, 107, 109, 112, 139, 142, 157
Gilsa, Colonel Leopold von 56, **60**, 69, 124
Godwin, Colonel Archibald C. **(57th North Carolina Infantry)** 52, 72, 79(n. 101), 92
Gordon, Brigadier General George H. 98-99, 130-131
Grafton, West Virginia 5
Greg, Captain, Acting Assistant Inspector-General, Colonel Carroll's Brigade 47
Greene, Brigadier General George S. 132, 133, 133(n. 197)
Greenland, West Virginia 5
Grubb, Captain Peter **(4th Ohio Infantry)** 37, **38**
Gum Springs, Virginia 20

H

Hamblin, Charles P. 104-105
Halleck, General in Chief Henry W. 22, 127
Hancock, Major General Winfield S. 23(n. 33), 24(n. 37), 28, 28(n. 43), **30**, 33, 46, 46(n. 69), 50, 82, 100, 102, 104, 106, 108, 110, 112, 114, 119, 132(n. 195), 142, 143, 152, 156, 157
Hanover Road 50
Harper's Ferry, West Virginia 11, 19
Harris, Colonel Andrew L. **(75th Ohio Infantry)** 56, **58**, 66, 69, 94(n. 131), 154
Harrison's Landing, Virginia 7, 8(n. 13)
Hays, Brigadier General Alexander 15, 20, **21**, 32, 35, 39, 43, 49, 105
Hays, Brigadier General Harry T. 52, **54**, 91, 109
Hills, Brigadier General C.W. 5
Hooker, Major General Joseph 12, 15(n. 19), 16, 18, 99, 100
Houghton, William **(14th Indiana Infantry)** 122, **123**
Howard, Major General Oliver O. 1, 15, 46, 47(n. 70), 63(n. 82), 74, 93, 96, **97**, 98, 99, 100, 102, 102(n. 145), 103, 104-107, 111, 111(n. 160), 112, 113, 114, 116, 118, 120, 122, 127, 129, 130, 132, 133, 139, 140, 141, 142, 144, 150, 152, 153, 154, 156, 159

Huber, A.H. 148, 149
Hunt, Brigadier General Henry J. Chief of Artillery, Army of the Potomac 132, 132(n. 195)
Huntington, Captain James F. 82, 125(n. 180)

J

Jackson, Lieutenant General Thomas J. "Stonewall" 1, 7, 56
James River 7
Jamestown, Maryland 24
Jefferies, Lemuel **(4th Ohio Infantry)** 19, 33, 94(n. 134)
Johnson, Major General Edward "Old Allegheny" 50, 50(n. 76), 52, 91

K

Kelley, Brigadier General B.F. 5
Kepler, William **(4th Ohio Infantry)** 18, 20, 27, 32(n. 45), 37, 42, 87, 89
Koenig, Captain Emil **(58th New York Infantry)** 74(n. 94), 76(n. 97)
Kimball, Brigadier General Nathan 3, 4, 7, 8, 8(n. 8), 11
Krzyzanowski, Colonel Wladimir 74, 76, 124

L

Lambert, George Washington **(14th Indiana Infantry)** 37
Landers, Brigadier General F.W. 7
Latimer, Major Joseph W. 50, 50(n. 75), 52
Lee, General Robert E. 3, 16, 100
Leesburg, Virginia 11, 20
Liberty, Maryland 24
Lincoln, Abraham, President of the United States 3, 5, 99(n. 142)
Lockwood, Lieutenant Colonel Jonathan **(7th West Virginia Infantry)** 32-33(n. 47), 89(n. 121)
Longstreet, Lieutenant General James 41, 50, 91
Lookout Valley, Tennessee 104
Lutz, Captain John **(107th Ohio Infantry)** 56(n. 79), 71
Lynch, James C. 127, 127(n. 186)

Mc

McAbee, Surgeon Harry M. **(4th Ohio Infantry)** 8(n. 13), **10**
McClellan, Major General George B. 3, 8(n. 13)
McClure, J.R. **(14th Indiana Infantry)** 125
McCook, Colonel R.L. 3
McDowell, Major General Irvin 7
McElroy, John 153
McKnight House, Gettysburg, Pennsylvania **73**

M

Malvern Hill, Virginia 7
Marye's Heights, Fredericksburg, Virginia 11
Mason, Colonel John S. 12, **13**
Meade, Major General George Gordon 15, 22, 23, 23(n. 33), 25-26, 28(n. 43), 99, 104, 105, 106, 110
Miller, Lieutenant J. Clyde **(153rd Pennsylvania Infantry)** 61(n. 81), 71-72
Monocacy Bridge, Maryland 22
Montgomerey, James Stuart 156
Moore, L. Eugene C. **(Batteries F and G, 1st Pennsylvania Light Artillery)** 69, 79-80, 150
Morgantown, West Virginia 5
Mount Jackson, Virginia 7
Mud March 12
Murdock, J.E. **(7th West Virginia Infantry)** 79-80(n. 104), 150
Myerhoff, Charles ("M") **(14th Indiana Infantry)** 114, 114(n. 166), 133, 133(n. 199), 154

N

National Tribune 1, 112, 113, 114, 116, 120, 122, 124, 125, 126, 131, 133, 134, 136, 137, 138, 140, 141, 142, 144, 145, 149, 150, 152, 153, 154
New Market, Virginia 7
Nickerson, Captain Azor H. **(8th Ohio Infantry)** 41
Norris, Corporal Isaac **(14th Indiana Infantry)** 87, 87(n. 114)
Norvell, Major J.M., Adjutant General, Third Division, Second Corps, Army of the Potomac 46, 105

O

Official Records 126, 131, 132, 134

"One Who Knows" 104, 106
Osborn, Major Thomas W. 63(n. 82), 127, **128**

P

Paris, Louis Philippe Albert d'Orleans, Comte de (Count of Paris) 118-119
Peach Orchard, Gettysburg, Pennsylvania 45(n. 65), 145
Peck, Lieutenant A.W. **(17th Connecticut Infantry)** 125, 126, 127, 130, 131-132, 133, 133-134(n. 200), 134, 135, 137-138, 139-141, 141(n. 212), 145, 154, 156
Petersburg, Virginia 5(n. 6)
Pfanz, Harry 50(n. 74), 60(n. 81), 157, 157(n. 248)
Poolesville, Maryland 22
Pope, Major General John 7, 12
Portland, West Virginia 5
Power's Hill, Gettysburg, Pennsylvania 28

R

Rapidan River 12
Rappahannock River 11, 12
Reid, Captain **(8th Ohio Infantry)** 44
Reid, Lieutenant John J. **(8th Ohio Infantry)** 113-114, 116, 120, 142
Rosecrans, Brigadier General William S. 3
Reynolds, Major General John F. 27, 126
Richmond, Virginia 16
Ricketts, Captain R. Bruce **(Batteries F and G, 1st Pennsylvania Light Artillery)** 2, 63, 69, 77, 77(n. 98), **78**, 109, 110, 110(n. 158), 134, 139
Rider, Alfred **(107th Ohio Infantry)** 71(n. 88)
Rodes, Major General Robert E. 91
Romney, West Virginia 5

S

Sauers, Richard 103(n. 148)
Sawyer, Lieutenant Colonel Franklin **(8th Ohio Infantry)** 23-24, 35, 39, 39(n.56), **40**, 41, 45, 49
Schimmelfennig, Brigadier General Alexander 131
Schurz, Major General Carl 74, **75**, 76, 76(n. 97), 96, 112, 124, 131(n. 193), 132, 134, 144

Second Bull Run, Battle of 15
"Second Corps" 111
Sedgwick, Major General John 126
Seminary Ridge, Gettysburg, Pennsylvania 33
Sharpsburg, Maryland 8
Shenandoah Valley, Virginia 7, 16
Sickles, Major General Daniel E. 39, 45(n. 65), 132
Sigel, Major General Franz 131
Slocum, Major General Henry 28(n. 43), 46(n. 69)
Smith, Colonel Orland 61, 129-130
Spotsylvania, Battle of 109
Stanton, Edwin M., Secretary of War 22
Steinwehr, Brigadier General Adolph von 61, **62**, 124, 129, 130
Stevens, Captain Greenlief T. **(5th Maine Battery)** 63
Stevens' Knoll, Gettysburg, Pennsylvania **73**
Stine, James Henry 142
Stuart, Major General J.E.B. 22
Sugar Loaf Mountain, Maryland 22
Sumner, Major General Edwin V. "Bull" 8, 11
Sunken Road, Battle of Antietam 8, 11
Sweet, Oney F. **(Batteries F and G, 1st Pennsylvania Light Artillery)** 79, 148
Sweetland, A.F. **(55th Ohio Infantry)** 151, 151(n. 233), 152, 152(n. 238), 156

T

Tate, Major Samuel **(6th North Carolina Infantry)** 92
Taneytown, Maryland 24(n. 36), 25, 28, 28(n. 43)
Taneytown Road 32-33(n. 47), 33, 47
Terre Haute, Indiana 3
Thurston, Corporal William **(Batteries F and G, 1st Pennsylvania Light Artillery)** 139-140, 141, 154
"Truth" 99, 102, 103, 103(n. 148), 104, 106
Tyler, Brigadier General Robert O. 79(n. 101)

U

Underwood, Colonel Adin B. **(33rd Massachusetts Infantry)** 116, **117**, 145(n. 221)
Union Forces
    Army of Occupation 3, 5

Army of the Potomac 2, 3, 8, 12, 56, 99, 139, 157
Army of the Shenandoah 109
Army of Virginia 12
Department of the Rappahannock 12
Union Corps
    First Corps **(Reynolds)** 122, 124, 145
    Second Corps **(Sumner)** 8
    Second Corps **(Couch)** 15, 15(n. 19)
    Second Corps **(Hancock)** 2, 3, 16, 23(n. 33), 24(n. 36), 33, 96, 105, 127, 158
    Third Corps **(Sickles)** 41
    Third Corps, Army of Virginia **(McDowell)** 12
    Tenth Corps, Department of the South **(Gilman)** 99
    Eleventh Corps **(Howard)** 1, 2, 33, 56, 69, 96, 98, 103, 104, 105, 106, 109, 111, 116, 122, 124, 126, 127, 129, 130, 131, 133, 136, 137, 138-139, 138(n. 208), 144, 145, 152, 153, 156, 158
    Twelfth Corps **(Slocum)** 99, 127, 130, 132(n. 196)
Union Divisions/Districts
    First Division, Eleventh Corps **(Barlow)** 52, 69, 72, 93, 96, 98, 104, 122, 133, 134, 141
    Second Division, Second Corps **(Gibbon)** 104, 105, 109
    Third Division, Second Corps **(French)** 12
    Third Division, Second Corps **(Hays)** 32-33(n. 47)
    Third Division, Third Corps **(Whipple)** 15
    Third Division, Eleventh Corps **(Schurz)** 113, 154
    Fourth Division, Second Corps **(Mott)** 108
    Division of the Atlantic 109
    Railroad District, Department of Western Virginia **(Kelley)** 5, 7
    Shields' Division, Department of the Rappahannock **(Shields)** 12
Union Brigades
    First Brigade, First Division, Eleventh Corps **(von Gilsa)** 56, **60**, 61(n. 81), 71, 72, **73**, 109, 110(n. 158), 117, 120, 124, 134, 144, 153
    First Brigade [Gibraltar Brigade], Second Division, Second Corps **(Carroll)** 2, 11-12, 15, 16, 18-20, 22-23, 24, 27, 28, 32, 32-33(n. 47), 41, 42, 50, 82, 83, 83(n. 111), **67**, 93, 94, 94-95(n. 134), 95, 96, 102, 104, 107-108, 110, 111, 111(n. 160), 112, 113, 114, 116, 118, 119, 122, 125, 132(n. 195), 133, 134, 136, 137, 138, 138(n. 208), 139, 140, 141-143, 144-145, 145(n. 221), 148, 149-150, 151, 152, 153-155, 156-157
    First Brigade, Second Division, Eleventh Corps **(Coster)** 76

211

First Brigade, Third Division, Second Corps **(Kimball)** 8, 8(n.13)
First Brigade, Third Division, Eleventh Corps **(von Amsberg)** 132-133
First Brigade, Landers' Division, Department of Western Virginia **(Kimball)** 7, 7(n. 10)
Second Brigade, First Division, Eleventh Corps **(Ames)** 56, 61(n. 81), 71, 76-77(n. 97), 118, 120, 133-134(n. 200), 134, 136, 139, 142, 144, 153, 154, 158
Second Brigade, Second Division, First Corps **(Baxter)** 113
Second Brigade [Philadelphia Brigade], Second Division, Second Corps **(Webb)** 43, 46(n. 69)
Second Brigade, Second Division, Eleventh Corps **(Smith)** 61, 136
Second Brigade, Third Division, Second Corps **(Smyth)** 41, 42, 43, 47
Second Brigade, Third Division, Third Corps **(Carroll)** 15, 15(n. 19)
Third Brigade, Second Division, Eleventh Corps **(Greene)** 132, 132(n. 196)
Third Brigade, Third Division, Second Corps **(Willard)** 41
Third Brigade, Army of Occupation **(McCook)** 5
Hills' Brigade, Army of Occupation **(Hills)** 5
Kimball's Independent Brigade, Second Corps **(Kimball)** 7
McCook's Advance Brigade, Army of Occupation **(McCook)** 3

Union Regiments
14th Connecticut Infantry Regiment 107
17th Connecticut Infantry Regiment 56, 69, 71, 94(n. 131), 118, 125, 127, 127(n. 185), 134, **135**, 136, 138, 141, 154, **161**
1st Delaware Infantry Regiment 11, 35, 107
82nd Illinois Infantry Regiment 132
14th Indiana Infantry Regiment 3, 7, 19, 24(n. 36), 43, 47, 79(n. 101), 83, **85, 86**, 87, 87(n. 114), 89, 91, 94(n. 134), 137, 137(n. 204), 138, 152, 152(n. 238), 154, 162, **163, 164**
33rd Massachusetts Infantry Regiment 61, 63, **64, 65**, 66, 82, 116, 145, **146**, 147, 148, **165**
12th New Jersey Infantry Regiment 107
24th New Jersey Infantry Regiment 11, 19(n. 25)
28th New Jersey Infantry Regiment 11, 18, 19(n. 25)
10th New York Infantry Battalion 107
41st New York Infantry Regiment 56, 56(n. 80), 61, **64, 65**, 66, **166**
45th New York Infantry Regiment 132, 132(n. 197)
54th New York Infantry Regiment 56, 56(n. 80), 71, **167**

58th New York Infantry Regiment 74, 76, 132
68th New York Infantry Regiment 56, 71, 72, 99(n. 141), **168**
108th New York Infantry Regiment 107
119th New York Infantry Regiment 75, 77, 132
134th New York Infantry Regiment 77, **169**
136th New York Infantry Regiment 77(n. 97)
157th New York Infantry Regiment 133
4th Ohio Infantry Regiment 3, 5, 5(n. 6), 7, 8, 8(n. 13), 11, 12, 19, 24(n. 36), 35, 37, 43, 45(n. 65), 47, **73**, **86**, 87, 89, 91, 92-93, 93(n. 127), 94, 94-95(n. 134), 138, 154, **171**, **172**
    Company A 5(n. 6)
    Company F 5(n. 6)
    Company G 37, 43, 94
    Company I 37, 43, 94
    Company K 5(n. 6)
8th Ohio Infantry Regiment 3, 5, 7, 11, 19, 32-33(n. 47), 39, 39(n. 56, n. 57), 41, 41(n. 59), 45-46, 47, 49
    Company A 41
    Company D 45
    Company I 41
25th Ohio Infantry Regiment 56, 56(n. 79), **59**, 69, 94(n. 131), 118, **173**, **174**
55th Ohio Infantry Regiment 137
61st Ohio Infantry Regiment 132, 133(n. 197)
67th Ohio Infantry Regiment 7(n. 10)
75th Ohio Infantry Regiment 56, 69, **173**, **174**
107th Ohio Infantry Regiment 56, 56(n. 79), **59**, 69, 71, 71(n. 88), 74, 93-94(n. 131)
27th Pennsylvania Infantry Regiment 76, **175**
71st Pennsylvania Infantry Regiment 46(n. 69), 104
73rd Pennsylvania Infantry Regiment 76, 76(n. 97), **176**
74th Pennsylvania Infantry Regiment 131(n. 193), 132
84th Pennsylvania Infantry Regiment 7(n. 10), 153
106th Pennsylvania Infantry Regiment 94, 94(n. 131), 96, 104, 127, 127(n. 185), 134, **135**, 136, **177**
153rd Pennsylvania Infantry Regiment 56, 56(n. 80), 61, **64**, **65**, 71-72, 99(n. 141), **178**
    Company A 61
    Company F 61
7th West Virginia Infantry Regiment 3, 5, 5(n. 8), **6**, 7, 19, 24(n. 36), 43-44, 47, **86**, 89, 91, 92, 92(n. 126), 95(n. 134), 139, 150, 152, 153(n. 238), 154, **182**

7th Wisconsin Infantry Regiment 120
Union Batteries
    5th Maine Battery, First Corps Artillery Brigade 63, **68**, 72, 148
    Battery A, 4th United States Artillery, Second Corps Artillery Brigade 453(n. 65)
    Battery B, 1st Pennsylvania Light Artillery, First Corps Artillery Brigade 77(n. 98), 179, **180**
    Battery B, 2nd Maine Light Artillery, First Corps Artillery Brigade 39
    Battery B, 4th United States Artillery, First Corps Artillery Brigade 63, 72, 120
    Batteries E and L, 1st New York Light Artillery, First Corps Artillery Brigade 63, 66, **73**
    Batteries F and G, 1st Pennsylvania Light Artillery, Third Volunteer Brigade, Artillery Reserve 63, 66, 77, 79-80, 79(n. 101), 82, 83, **85**, **86**, **88**, 94(n. 132), 96, 122, 125, 139, 140, 141, 142, **146**, **147**, 148, 150, 151, 152, 153, 154, 156, 158, **181**
    Battery I, 1st New York Light Artillery, Eleventh Corps Artillery Brigade 63, 66, 71, 72, 74, 74(n. 94), 76, 76(n. 97), 77, 79, 83(n. 111), 94, 96, 111, 112, 118, 122, 125, 132, 139, 140, 141, 142, 144, 146, 150, 151, 152, 153, 158, **170**
    Battery I, 1st United States Artillery, Second Corps Artillery Brigade 32, 32-33(n. 47), 37, 42, 45(n. 65)
Union Bridge, Maryland 24
Uniontown, Maryland 24
United States Ford 12

V

Virginia Peninsula 7

W

Wadsworth, Brigadier General James S. 96, 132, 145
Wainwright, Colonel Charles 63(n. 82), 66, **67**, 72, 77, 77(n. 98), 91
Wainwright Avenue, Gettysburg, Pennsylvania 73, 127(n. 185), **146**, **147**, 152(n. 238)
Washington, DC 16
Webb, Brigadier General Alexander S. 126

Weidrich, Captain Michael **(Battery I, First New York Light Artillery)** 76(n. 97)
Wheatfield, Gettysburg, Pennsylvania 144-145
Wheeling, West Virginia 5
Whipple, Brigadier General Amiel W. 15(n. 19)
Whittier, Lieutenant Edward N. **(5th Maine Battery)** 66
Whitzel, John T. **(7th West Virginia Infantry) 90**
Wickham, Colonel C.P. **(55th Ohio Infantry)** 151
Wickham, W.S. **(55th Ohio Infantry)** 137, 138, 151(n. 235), 156
Wilderness, Battle of 108
Williams, Brigadier General Seth, Assistant Adjutant-General, Army of the Potomac 15(n. 19), 23(n. 33), 105
Winchester, Virginia 7
Woodruff, Lieutenant George A. **(Battery I, 1st United States Artillery)** 32, 37
Woodstock, Virginia 7
Wright, Owen **(14th Indiana Infantry)** 138-139, 138(n. 208), 141

Y

Young, Jesse Bowman **(84th Pennsylvania Infantry)** 153
Young, Captain Peter **(107th Ohio Infantry)** 56(n. 79), 71, 74, 74(n. 93)

Z

Ziegler's Grove, Gettysburg, Pennsylvania 32, 32-33(n. 47)